HIGH DESERT DEPLOYMENT

NAVY COLORS ON DISPLAY AT NAS FALLON

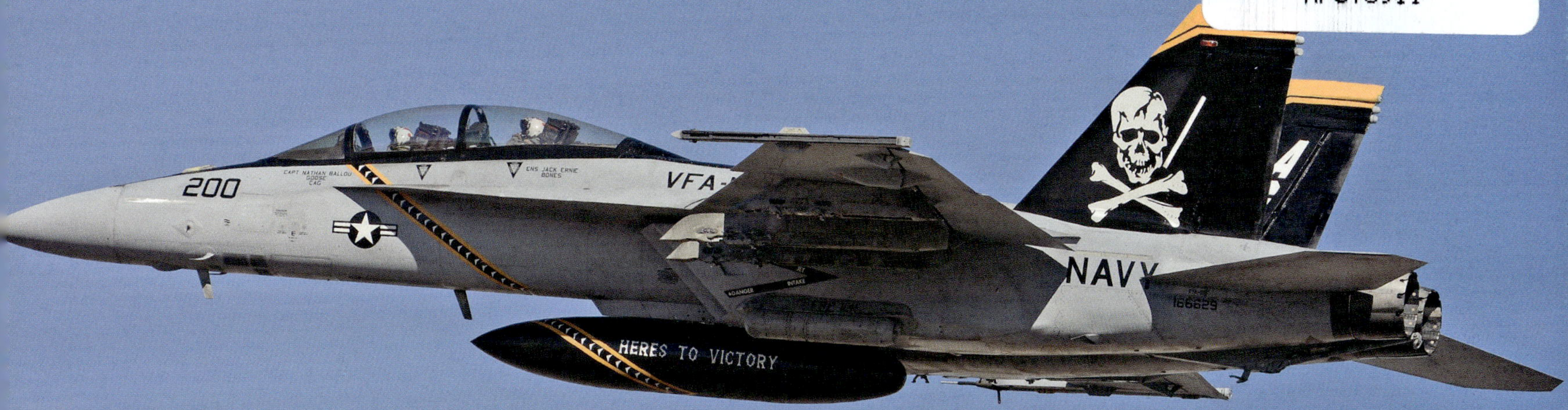

JIM DUNN & NICHOLAS A. VERONICO

KEY Books

Front cover image: To mark its 60th anniversary in 2015, the "Diamondbacks" of VFA-102 chose F/A-18F 166917/102 to be given a special scheme to honor the occasion. Some of the most colorful schemes given to Navy aircraft can be found on those assigned to Carrier Air Wing Five (CVW-5), which is based in Japan as the only forward deployed air wing in the Navy. The Diamondbacks have been stationed in Japan with CVW-5 since 2003. (Jim Dunn)

Title page image: Several months prior to an at-sea deployment by a carrier air wing, most squadrons assigned will make two work-up deployments to Naval Air Station (NAS) Fallon. The first of these is the Strike Fighter Advanced Readiness Program (SFARP), a three-week course to sharpen the skills of the four strike fighter squadrons assigned to each air wing, while the second deployment is the five-week Air Wing Fallon that includes all of the air wing squadrons. The CAG-bird of the "Jolly Rogers" of VFA-103, F/A-18F 166629/200, departs on an SFARP sortie from Fallon on October 28, 2021. (Jim Dunn)

Contents page image: Two of the longest runways in the Navy, three ranges that allow for both air combat maneuvering (ACM) and the use of live ordinance delivery, four of the Navy's premier "schoolhouses," including the famous TOP GUN, and year-round flying weather all combine to make NAS Fallon one of the busiest facilities in naval aviation. (Jim Dunn)

Back cover image: Paramount Pictures paid to have two Super Hornets painted with special markings to be used in the *Top Gun: Maverick* motion picture released in May 2022. The single-seat F/A-18E that received most of the screen time is now flying as Blue Angels Number One, while F/A-18F 165796/00 is still based with the Naval Aviation Warfighting Development Center (NAWDC) at NAS Fallon. This aircraft was fitted with up to six cameras in the rear cockpit to capture the actors during the flying scenes, many of which originated from Fallon. (Jim Dunn)

The authors wish to thank Zip Upham, NAS Fallon PAO, for his generous assistance in the preparation of this book.

Published by Key Books
An imprint of Key Publishing Ltd
PO Box 100
Stamford
Lincs PE9 1XQ

www.keypublishing.com

The right of Jim Dunn and Nicholas A. Veronico to be identified as the authors of this book has been asserted in accordance with the Copyright, Designs and Patents Act 1988 Sections 77 and 78.

Copyright © Jim Dunn and Nicholas A. Veronico, 2023

ISBN 978 1 80282 365 3

All rights reserved. Reproduction in whole or in part in any form whatsoever or by any means is strictly prohibited without the prior permission of the Publisher.

Typeset by SJmagic DESIGN SERVICES, India.

CONTENTS

Foreword by Capt. Gil Rud, USN ret.		4
Chapter One	An Air Station and its Mission	5
Chapter Two	Air Wing Fallon	17
Chapter Three	Roll Call of Squadrons	36
Chapter Four	Saints and Other Sinners	96
Chapter Five	Sentinels of the Past	115

FOREWORD

As a former Light Attack pilot and a veteran of multiple deployments to NAS Fallon, I thoroughly enjoyed *High Desert Deployment*. It will bring back great memories for the thousands of Naval Aviators and sailors who have trained in the high desert over the years. It will also bring you up-to-date on the composition of today's air wings and training activities.

NAS Fallon is where all nine air wings train prior to deploying on their respective aircraft carriers. The motto of the Naval Strike Warfare Center is: "Train the way you fight and fight the way you train." This book showcases how NAS Fallon allows air wings to do exactly that.

During the Vietnam War, we were able to practice massive, multi-plane Alpha Strikes, including launching and landing as though we were flying from an aircraft carrier. Today, Fallon is where the modern, complex, super-capable air wings mold into a cohesive/lethal fighting force.

As you read this book, you will marvel at the incredible photos of both the aircraft flown by the current air wings, as well as the legacy aircraft that are on display in Heritage Park on the base.

This expertly researched work serves as a great reference and source of information about current carrier air wings. The squadron histories and their capabilities are described in just the right amount of detail.

If you have wondered whether our Navy is ready to face current and future threats, you will feel a lot more confident after you read *High Desert Deployment*.

Gil Rud ("Duster," Captain, USN, ret.)
 Commanding Officer, USS *Constellation* (CVA-64)
 Commanding Officer, U.S. Navy Flight Demonstration Squadron, Blue Angels
 Commanding Officer, VA-192 "World Famous Golden Dragons"

CHAPTER ONE
AN AIR STATION AND ITS MISSION

Not receiving full naval air station status until January 1, 1972, NAS Fallon was still a remote and sparsely populated base when this flight of four T-28B Trojans from the "Boomers" of VT-27 flew over in the mid-1970s. On the right is Hangar 1 and MAT 1, which is the designated area for visiting air wings when conducting operations during deployments to Fallon. (NAS Fallon archives)

Naval air stations, like the squadrons that call them home, develop an identity and history over years that will have a lasting impact on the career and lives of those that serve there. For Naval Air Station (NAS) Fallon, that legacy ranks it at the forefront of naval aviation.

NAS Fallon is approximately 55 miles east of the city of Reno. The Civil Aeronautic Authority, the forerunner of today's Federal Aviation Administration, selected Fallon as a site for a future airport in March 1939, and negotiated with Churchill County to lease acreage for the airfield. The airbase came about in the early days of World War Two, when the US Army Air Forces realized it may need bases to defend against a Japanese invasion of the West Coast. A number of additional sites were selected on the eastern side of the Sierra Nevada mountain range including Lovelock, Minden, and Winnemucca – all within 130 miles of Fallon.

Fallon boasts 242 sunny days on average and only seven inches of snow per year as it lies in the rain shadow of the Sierra Nevada mountains, making the location ideal for flight training operations. Needing expanded training facilities, the US Army Corps of Engineers constructed two 5,200ft-long runways, which were finished in December 1942. Although the Army Air Forces did not occupy the airfield, the US Navy took up the lease in August 1943.

During late 1943, a third runway was constructed and a torpedo and gunnery range was opened at Pyramid Lake, less than 60 air miles to the northwest. Naval Auxiliary Air Station (NAAS) Fallon was commissioned on June 10, 1944. The plan was to base one carrier air group (CAG) at the air station; however, a second CAG was also able to be accommodated on the field. Following the conclusion of World War Two, NAAS Fallon was placed in reserve status on June 1, 1946.

Partially reactivated for the Korean War, Fallon became an Auxiliary Landing Field and its bombing and gunnery ranges were used extensively as squadrons prepared for battle with the North Koreans. After the armistice was signed that divided the Korean Peninsula at the 38th parallel, Fallon was again commissioned as an NAAS on October 1, 1953. Although the torpedo-dropping mission had been deleted, the air station provided gunnery, bomb and rocket training ranges for the fleet.

The following month, November 1953, a new 10,000ft runway was completed and the air field was named to honor LCdr. Bruce A. Van Voorhis, who grew up in Fallon. Van Voorhis was awarded the Medal of Honor, posthumously, for his single-plane attack on Greenwich Island (Kapingamarangi Atoll), the southernmost island in Micronesia. Flying a US Navy PB4Y-1 Liberator, Van Voorhis and his crew made six bombing and strafing runs, destroying a radio station, anti-aircraft emplacements and three moored seaplanes, and downed one fighter in the air. On the final pass, Van Voorhis dropped bombs that destroyed his target; however, the blast knocked the Liberator out of the air. It crashed into the lagoon and the crew of ten perished. Nine were honored with posthumous Distinguished Flying Crosses and another with the Navy Cross.

Nineteen years later, NAAS Fallon was transitioned to a full naval air station on February 9, 1972. At the ceremony to commemorate Fallon's becoming a naval air station, a 504-man bachelor enlisted quarters and a runway extension to 14,000ft, the longest in the Navy, was marked. The Navy immediately had to placate local miners, ranchers and private pilots, who were concerned with the air and ground restrictions put in place to accommodate various training ranges in the area. At the time, the Navy ranges covered more than 500,000 acres.

Base Consolidation for Improved Training

In 1993, the US Navy had been operating its fast-moving jets from NAS Miramar, approximately 25 miles north of NAS North Island, both in the San Diego, California, metropolitan area. The US Marine Corps, meanwhile, had established two bases at the southern end of the Los Angeles basin at El Toro and Tustin, approximately 75 miles north of San Diego. Marine Corps fixed-wing aircraft were operated from Marine Corps Air Station (MCAS) El Toro, while MCAS Tustin was home to rotary wing operations.

Residential growth in the Orange County area where the Marine Corps aviation units were based had encroached to the borders of both air stations. Miramar, on the other hand, enjoyed the Scripps Ranch open space to the east and the Pacific Ocean less than seven miles to the west. Although not ideal, the buffer zone around Miramar made the base a good neighbor and the servicemen and women from the base certainly fed the local economy.

In the years following the end of the Cold War (marked officially on December 26, 1991), there was a huge drawdown of staffing and facilities within the US military. Congress authorized the Department of Defense to consolidate bases, eliminate redundant facilities and increase operational training and readiness. When the 1993 Base Realignment and Closure (BRAC) committee looked at operations in the Southland, it was easy to see that encroachment had spelled the end of Marine aviation in Orange County. Simultaneously, all Navy F-14 squadrons were transferred from the west coast to NAS Oceana, Virginia, leaving NAS Miramar in search of a mission.

Out of the BRAC committee report came the recommendation that Navy training at Miramar and its signature TOP GUN school be moved to NAS Fallon, Nevada, and MCAS El Toro and Tustin be closed with the units moved south to Miramar. Change is never easy, but looking back upon the consolidation, this has turned out to be the ideal solution. The Marines now have fixed- and rotary-wing training on one base that is close to the coast and the desert training areas in the eastern part of California, and the Navy's training operations have been consolidated at NAS Fallon, Nevada. New facilities have been constructed at Fallon to accommodate the base's expanded role, and the base's nearby air-to-air, gunnery and electronic warfare ranges provide a training environment where each of the different aircraft within a carrier air group can operate together, simulating real-life combat.

Through various iterations, today Navy training at Fallon is known as the Naval Aviation Warfighting Development Center (NAWDC) or "Naw-Dik." Within NAWDC are 11 directorates, each responsible for training naval and marine air and ground crews to the highest state of combat readiness. Those directorates are as follows:

- The Information Warfare Directorate provides training for both officer and enlisted personnel in three areas: Air Wing Intelligence, the Targeting Division, and Command Information Systems.
- The NAWDC Operations department coordinates all activities of aircraft, airspace, and operations within the Fallon Range Training Complex (FRTC).
- The Maintenance Department maintains NAWDC's fleet and adversary aircraft's weapons and systems for its training mission.
- The Strike Directorate teaches advanced tactics, techniques, and procedures to specific standards to all levels of Navy and Marine warfighters, including at all levels of force integration.
- Within NAWDC's Strike Directorate is the Joint Close-Air Support (JCAS) Division, which trains Naval Special Warfare and Riverine Group fighters. Strike Directorate's JCAS has also trained US Navy Fixed and Rotary Wing Forward-Air Controllers, along with US Army Special Operations, and US Marine Corps Air and Naval Gunfire Liaison Officers.

- TOP DOME, the Carrier Airborne Early Warning Weapons School, which is the E-2 Hawkeye school where airborne tactical command and control and the Hawkeye Weapons and Tactics Instructors are taught.
- TOP GUN is the Navy's Fighter Weapons School and where the Strike Fighter Tactics Instructor course is taught. Graduates are air intercept controllers, adversary instructors and strike fighter tacticians, who leave TOP GUN and disseminate those skills to the fleet.
- HAVOC is the call sign for the Airborne Electronic Attack Weapons School, focusing on EA-18G Growler tactics. HAVOC graduates bring the latest information and tactics to fleet squadrons to maintain peak electronic-warfare readiness.
- The service's Rotary Wing Weapons School flies the Sikorsky Seahawk helicopter and teaches helicopter tactics to sea-based squadrons as well as providing training at the Mountain Flying School and in search-and-rescue procedures.
- One of the most important directorates at NAWDC is the Safety Department, concerned with safe ground and flight operations.
- The Tomahawk Land Attack Missile (TLAM) department works to provide training for carrier air wings and other commands in the tactics of using the Tomahawk missile and how to integrate the missile into the carrier strike force.

Applying Tactics

NAWDC's ranges enable all aircraft types in a carrier air wing to train together and practice the tactics and procedures needed for integrated strike warfare. Practicing how the EA-18 Growler, E-2 Hawkeye, and MH-60 Seahawk support F/A-18s and F-35s in both the strike and air-superiority roles can be flown over Fallon's ranges in scenarios close to actual combat. To accomplish such training, each organization needs a safe, dedicated, air and ground space to apply the tactics and procedures learned in the classroom.

To that end, NAWDC manages 12,256-square nautical miles of airspace and controls about 232,000 acres of land for target ranges, air-to-air engagement areas, radio and instrument ranges, and an electronic warfare range for HAVOC school operations – known as the Dixie Valley Training Area. The range complex is approximately 140 statute miles north to south at its widest point and 200 miles east to west. There are four ranges known as the Bravo Ranges – B-16, B-17, B-19, and B-20 – where ordnance drops and live fire training occurs. Supersonic flight is allowed over the majority of the range above 30,000ft (Flight Level 300) and in certain areas as low as 11,000ft above sea level (NAS Fallon is at 3,934ft).

The colors and markings of US Navy and Marine Corps aircraft are ever-changing. One of the best places to see the wide variety of markings is when air wings travel to the NAWDC at NAS Fallon, Nevada, to prepare for deployment.

Opposite: This view from the Fallon tower overlooking Van Voorhis Field in 2007 shows the expansion of the air wing area now encompassing both MAT 1 and 2. Today, this view is obscured by the ever-increasing number of sun shelters that are being erected on both the air wing and NAWDC ramps. The small tower seen between those two ramps gained fame as the sight of the famous tower buzz job by Maverick in the original *Top Gun* movie. Of note are the yellow fuel trucks that are a constant presence as they deliver much of the 60 million gallons of jet fuel used for flight operations at Fallon each year. (Jim Dunn)

In the late 1970s, activity at the now-designated NAS Fallon began to steadily increase as more air wings were deployed to the high desert base for training. The bombing ranges were one of the areas seeing an increased tempo, as can be viewed here on November 2, 1978, as A-7E 158021/400, the CAG-bird of the "Dambusters" of VA-195, readies for a flight to drop a load of MK-82 500lb bombs. This Corsair II went on to serve in the Hellenic Air Force from 1994 until its retirement in 2014. (Peter B. Lewis)

The early 1980s saw the Navy begin construction on the facilities that became the Naval Strike Warfare Center in 1984. Colorful aircraft of this era, such as F-14A 159846/201 from the "Blacklions" of VF-213, seen at Fallon on November 6, 1980, would help put the base at the forefront of naval aviation training. The glory years of this Tomcat would be cut short by two operational accidents that saw the two crewmembers killed by an inadvertent ejection on January 13, 1986, followed by the loss of the aircraft itself on February 14, 1986, when it ran out of fuel during an extended patrol over the Philippine Sea. (William T. Larkins)

No doubt the most recognizable, and by far the most popular adornment given to a military aircraft is a fearsome shark mouth. Originated on Royal Air Force (RAF) P-40s during the North Africa campaign early in the war, the shark mouth was made famous by the American Volunteer Group "Flying Tigers" in China shortly after America entered World War Two. Some squadrons have continued this tradition, however, it has been rarely seen on US Navy Super Hornets. The most recent exception is F/A-18E 166828/400, the CAG-bird for the "Vigilantes" of VFA-151. (Jim Dunn)

At certain times, such as an anniversary or special event in its history, a squadron will designate an aircraft to receive a scheme or markings to commemorate the occasion. *Splash Two*, F/A-18F 166850/107 from the "Black Aces" of VFA-41, marks August 19, 1981, when two of the squadron's F-14s scored the first aerial victories in the history of the Tomcat. Featured are the names of Squadron CO CDR Henry M. "Hank" Kleemann and his radar intercept officer (RIO) Lt. David "DJ" Venlet, who were flying F-14A 160403/102 when they shot down one of the two Libyan Su-22 Fitters that VF-41 scored that day. (Jim Dunn)

High Desert Deployment: Navy Colors on Display at NAS Fallon

Left: For many years, the "Eagles" of VFA-115 have paid tribute to members of the New York Fire Department who gave their lives on September 11, 2001. On the squadron's CAG-bird, F/A-18E 166859/300, is a memorial to the fallen first responders from Engine 54, Truck 4, Battalion 9, "The Pride of Midtown." (Jim Dunn)

Below and opposite: If a second aircraft in a squadron is given some color, it is likely because it has been assigned to the Commanding Officer (CO) of the squadron. Designated with a modex number ending in 01, the squadron's CO may decide to have a little, or a lot of color applied to his aircraft. Looking back on the days of the Legacy Hornet, F/A-18A 163135/401, from the "River Rattlers" of VFA-204, displays squadron colors rivaling that of the unit's CAG-bird, while Super Hornet F/A-18E 168911/401 from the "Golden Warriors" of VFA-87 is closer to the norm, with its squadron logo receiving the most color. (Jim Dunn)

The introduction of the Lockheed F-35C Lightning II has led to a new training syllabus called Air Wing Fallon, which is the final four-week deployment before the air wings join their carrier for the composite training unit exercise. If the first CAG-bird in this new era of the F-35C Lightning II is any indication, the future is going to be a colorless one. The "Argonauts" of VFA-147 is the first carrier air wing squadron in the Navy to go operational, and F-35C 169632/400 displays no color and very few markings on its stealthy surface. It can only be hoped that the squadrons not assigned the F-35C will continue the colorful tradition of the CAG-bird long into the future. (Jim Dunn)

CHAPTER TWO
AIR WING FALLON

Activity is high as its "all hands on deck" for the "Stingers" of VFA-113 as they prepare to launch their five F/A-18E Super Hornets from MAT 2 for a late afternoon go during a Strike Fighter Advanced Readiness Program (SFARP) deployment on October 26, 2022. Assigned to CVW-2, the Stingers would be joined on this SFARP mission by other Super Hornets from the "Bounty Hunters" of VFA-2, the "Golden Dragons" of VFA-192, and four EA-18G Growlers from the "Gauntlets" of VAQ-136. (Jim Dunn)

In 2023, there are nine carrier air wings, four based on ships with the Atlantic Fleet [CVW-1 on board USS *Harry S. Truman* (CVN-75); CVW-3, USS *Dwight D. Eisenhower* (CVN-69); CVW-7, USS *George H.W. Bush* (CVN-77); CVW-8, USS *Gerald R. Ford* (CVN-78)] and five as part of the Pacific Fleet [CVW-2, USS *Carl Vinson* (CVN-70); CVW-5, USS *Ronald Reagan* (CVN-76); CVW-9, USS *Abraham Lincoln* (CVN-72); CVW-11, USS *Theodore Roosevelt* (CVN-71); CVW-17, USS *Nimitz* (CVN-68)]. The Navy's two remaining carriers, the USS *George Washington* (CVN-73) and USS *John C. Stennis* (CVN-74), are currently undergoing maintenance and refueling at Newport News Shipbuilding, Newport News, Virginia.

The carrier air wing is, essentially, a temporary tenant of the aircraft carrier. The commander of the air wing, known as the "CAG" (a hold-over from the term Commander Air Group before they were Air Wings), in turn, reports to the aircraft carrier's captain who is in overall command of the ship and its operations. The CAG is the commander of the air wing's component squadrons, both fixed and rotary wing, as well as the transport squadron detachment.

Each squadron will have an aircraft designated as the "CAG-bird" that will carry a modex ending in 00, such as the E-2 Hawkeye squadron's CAG-bird will carry the modex 600. In turn, the squadron commander's aircraft will have a modex ending in 01, thus their Hawkeye will be 601. Typically, the CAG-bird will be adorned with that squadron's colors and become the "Flagship" for the squadron, provided that the CAG approves of the scheme. The squadron commander's aircraft may also have some color applied, but it is almost always to a much lesser extent. The remaining aircraft within each squadron, both fixed- and rotary-wing, will be painted in standard low-visibility markings.

One additional aircraft within the squadron may also receive some colorful marking in order to commemorate a special event or anniversary the squadron wishes to celebrate. Aside from looks, these colorful markings bring attention to the squadron that allows its members to point with pride to their aircraft and promote a sense of *esprit de corps* within the squadron. That pride will lead to members performing at a higher level, and as the old saying goes, "A good looking aircraft just seems to fly better."

The demands of training and deployment, aircraft squadron assignments, and maintenance all take a toll on the paint schemes an aircraft wears. The colors of the CAG and squadron commanders' aircraft can also be removed on board ship should a wartime situation occur. Returning to its shore station or receiving depot-level maintenance will present the squadron with an opportunity to apply new markings, adding another colorful era to the squadron's history.

At NAS Fallon itself, some of the adversary aircraft at NAWDC wear modified Soviet-bloc paint schemes, including the station's helicopters. When the aggressors of Fighter Squadron Composite (VFC)-13 "Fighting Saints" took delivery of its first F-16C Block 32, that jet was wearing the two-tone gray Have Glass V (Have Glass, fifth generation) scheme that incorporates new, radar-absorbing paint materials. Perhaps with some luck, these new aircraft of VFC-13 will someday feature some of the special color schemes that made their aircraft so unique.

Opposite: Most operational days of an air wing deployment will feature multiple mass launches involving the four strike fighter squadrons (VFA) as well as the electronic attack squadron (VAQ) and the airborne command and control squadron (VAW). The number of aircraft in each launch can vary greatly, as can the number of aircraft that each squadron contributes to that particular mission profile. Stretching the full width of MAT 2, this mix of a dozen F/A-18E and F/A-18F Super Hornets await clearance to begin the launch sequence. (Jim Dunn)

Opposite and right: Prior to taking the line for launch, each aircraft would spend time in the Combat Aircraft Loading Area (CALA) where the squadron's ordnance crew, the red-shirted crew on an aircraft carrier deck, will upload the required ordnance for that sortie's mission profile. In the CALA, crews can load a wide range of weapons, from air-to-air AIM-9 Sidewinders and AIM-120 Advanced Medium-Range Air-to-Air Missiles (AMRAAMs), to air-to-ground precision guided missiles such as the AGM-88 High-speed Anti-Radiation Missile (HARM). Dumb bombs, practice bombs and various sensors for use over the three Fallon ranges are also loaded before the aircraft return to their parking area. (Jim Dunn)

Below: A mass launch from the air wing will bring a corresponding response from opposing forces. In this case, four VFC-13 F-5Ns and a pair of F-16As from NAWDC stand ready to launch on Runway 13L. Adversary forces can be small or large depending on the mission profile, and the types of aircraft can include Super Hornets from NAWDC and other Navy squadrons, as well as aggressor aircraft from civilian contractors. (Jim Dunn)

Left and below: Night launches bring an added element of risk to the crews charged with getting the mission aircraft ready. There can be no more dangerous workplace than the flight deck of an aircraft carrier, and nightfall only increases that danger. These deployments will give the crews some additional training and experience working at night in preparation for their next cruise. (Jim Dunn)

Regardless of the time of the launches, the E-2 Hawkeyes and their crews are likely to be the first out and the last ones back. Each sortie will average between two and four hours of flight time, but with pre-mission planning, aircraft preparations and checks and the post-flight debrief, it makes for a long day for these crews. Seen here on May 20, 2019, this crew from the "Seahawks" of VAW-126 takes the CAG-bird E-2D 168275/600 out for a two-and-a-half-hour mission supporting the CVW-1 air wing. (Jim Dunn)

NAWDC also has Hawkeyes assigned to support their activities that include the famous Fighter Weapons School (TOP GUN) and Strike Fighter Tactics Instructor Course, as well as the lesser-known Carrier Airborne Early Warning Weapons School (TOP DOME) and its Hawkeye Weapons and Tactics Instructor Course. Trying to beat sundown, NAWDC E-2C 164112/600 makes an early evening return home to Fallon. (Jim Dunn)

Right and below: Since it became operational in 1972, the Grumman EA-6B Prowler would call Fallon's MAT 1 home during air wing deployments to the base. This would begin to change in 2009, when the first Boeing EA-18G Growler entered operational service, with the Prowler finally ending its air wing career in 2014. At present, there are 15 VAQ Squadrons that include one Fleet Replacement Squadron, one Reserve Squadron, five Expeditionary Squadrons and eight Carrier Air Wing Squadrons, with VAQ-144 in the process of becoming operational. The "Patriots" of VAQ-140 are currently assigned to CVW-7, and home-based at NAS Whidbey Island, Washington. (Jim Dunn)

High Desert Deployment: Navy Colors on Display at NAS Fallon

Left and below: This happy pair of "Wizards" from VAQ-133 step from their EA-18G Growler for a post-mission debrief after what must have been a very successful sortie. Success is due in large part to the training aircrew receive, and for Growler crews, NAWDC's Airborne Electronic Attack Warfare School is their TOP GUN. Known as HAVOC, for the effect the Growlers and their crews inflict on the enemy's radars and communications, this school and subsequent follow-on deployments to Fallon maintain the decided advantage held by these aircrew. NAWDC's EA-18G 168902/500 serves as the school's lead Growler in this image from August 2022. (Jim Dunn)

The "Vikings" of VAQ-129 have been the only training or Fleet Replacement Squadron throughout the history of the Prowler and Growler. Navy, Marine Corps, U.S. Air Force (USAF) and Royal Australian Air Force aircrews receive their introduction and training in Growler operations from VAQ-129 instructors belonging to those four services as well as from the RAF. With 55 Growlers assigned, such as EA-18G 169146/521 seen here in October 2021, the Vikings are no strangers when it comes to deployments to Fallon. Of note on this Growler is that the pilot carries the rank of Flight Lieutenant. (Jim Dunn)

To support land forces, the Navy operates five expeditionary VAQ squadrons that are deployable anywhere in the world from their home of NAS Whidbey Island, Washington. In April 2022, the Navy proposed to deactivate all five squadrons, VAQ-131 "Lancers," VAQ-132 "Scorpions," VAQ-134 "Garudas," VAQ-135 "Black Ravens," and VAQ-138 "Yellow Jackets," beginning in fiscal year 2024. All 25 EA-18G Growlers would be sent to the Aerospace Maintenance and Regeneration Group (AMARG), Davis-Monthan Air Force Base (AFB), Arizona, for storage. Since these squadrons are not assigned to a carrier air wing, their deployments to Fallon are less frequent. Seen here in May 2018 are EA-18G 168765/530, the color Growler for the Garudas of VAQ-134, and EA-18G 168259/520 from the Black Ravens of VAQ-135, wearing a new scheme after returning from a long deployment at bases throughout the Pacific in October 2021. (Jim Dunn)

Also no strangers to deployments to Fallon are Marine squadrons such as Marine All-Weather Fighter Attack Squadron 533 "Hawks." The ranges at Fallon offer this squadron opportunities to hone their skills in close air support, air interdiction, and aerial reconnaissance. Training areas for these missions do not exist near the unit's East Coast home base at Marine Corps Air Station (MCAS) Beaufort, South Carolina. The squadron's CAG-bird, F/A-18D 164957/00, is seen heading to one of the ranges, carrying a AN/AAQ-28(V) Litening Pod on its centerline, an AGM-88 HARM and an AIM-9 Sidewinder air-to-air missile on its left wingtip. (Jim Dunn)

Over the years, besides supporting air wing deployments, NSAWC/NAWDC has provided support to Navy Seal Teams that deploy for training in the high desert environment surrounding NAS Fallon. They also conduct the Rotary Wing Weapons School (RWWS), known as "Seawolf," and the Navy's Mountain Flying School. The schemes worn by NSAWC/NAWDC helicopters have been many and varied, from the former black helicopters, such as SH-60F 164092/70, to the current desert scheme of MH-60S 167817/75, and this lineup from June 1, 2022, that features the "Gecko" MH-60S 167822/73 in the foreground. (Jim Dunn)

Each carrier air wing has a pair of rotary wing squadrons assigned to it; one Helicopter Sea Combat Squadron (HSC) that operates the MH-60S Sea Hawk, and one Helicopter Maritime Strike Squadron (HSM) that operates the MH-60R Sea Hawk. While deployed at Fallon, the helicopter squadrons conduct operations from the airfield's MAT 7, as seen here with MH-60S 168569/15 from the "Chargers" of HSC-14 at the head of this lineup. (Jim Dunn)

The primary mission for the "Black Knights" of HSC-4 is anti-surface warfare, and, as can be seen here on MH-60S 168531/612, they can bring some firepower to the fight. Unofficially known as the "Knighthawk," the MH-60S can carry a variety of weapons, which on this sortie had an M197 20mm three-barrel cannon on the left pylon and an M261 launcher with 19 2.75in. rockets on the right pylon. The HSC squadrons also perform combat search and rescue (CSAR), special operations support, mine countermeasures and vertical replenishment missions. (Jim Dunn)

For the HSM squadrons, such as the "Swamp Foxes" of HSM-74, the primary missions are anti-submarine warfare, and overwater search and rescue. The latter includes the important role of plane guard while the carrier is conducting air operations. Equipped with a nose-mounted, forward-looking infrared (FLIR) turret, the Swamp Foxes MH-60R CAG-bird, 168090/700, makes its approach after a wintry mission over Fallon. (Jim Dunn)

NAWDC is slated to receive six F-35C Lightning IIs over the next few years. The second of those F-35Cs is 168844/201, seen here departing for a mission on October 28, 2021. At present, NAWDC has a quota of three F-35Cs; however, it is often forced to borrow an aircraft from squadrons such as VX-9 at China Lake to fulfill mission requirements. (Jim Dunn)

The Marine Corps will transition four squadrons from Legacy Hornets to the F-35C for assignments to carrier air wings. In 2021, the Black Knights of VMFA-314 completed its workups at Fallon prior to going aboard the USS *Abraham Lincoln* with CVW-9, becoming the first Marine F-35C squadron to join an air wing for an operational deployment. Returning to Fallon on June 2, 2021, F-35C 169633/300 leads 169703/310 and 169639/303 back from a sortie over the Fallon ranges. (Jim Dunn)

CHAPTER THREE
ROLL CALL OF SQUADRONS

Aircraft carriers operate on a three-year cycle of maintenance; a work-up phase, then an overseas deployment lasting approximately eight months, followed by homeporting where the post-deployment maintenance cycle begins again. When the air wings return to the continental United States, each of the squadrons is busy on-boarding new crewmembers, training, and flying in various exercises. When squadrons of the air wings deploy on board the carrier, all of the squadrons are again flying as a unit. To refresh each of the units in how to operate as a wing, all of the carrier air wing's assigned squadrons will arrive at NAWDC for the final work-up prior to a combat deployment.

NAS Fallon is the only air station and range complex that can accommodate and train an entire carrier air wing at one time. A carrier air wing typically consists of four strike fighter squadrons (VFA or VMFA), one electronic attack squadron (VAQ), one airborne early-warning squadron (VAW), one helicopter sea combat squadron (HSC), a helicopter maritime strike squadron (HSM), and a fleet logistics support squadron detachment (VRC).

Early into the deployment to Fallon, the strike fighter crews flying F/A-18 Super Hornets and F-35 Lightning IIs will begin working with the E-2 Hawkeye crews to refresh the vital skills required to exercise command and control during airborne missions in hostile airspace, or in defense of the carrier strike group.

The wing's electronic warfare EA-18G will also be integrated into the training with the strike fighters and Hawkeyes to form a cohesive strike package. In the airborne battlespace, Growlers protect strike aircraft by denying the enemy the ability to communicate and use its defensive radars to track and target the strike force, with the Fallon ranges playing an import part in this training. Growlers carry both the AGM-88 High-speed Anti-Radiation Missile (HARM), and the AGM-88E Advanced Anti-Radiation Guided Missile (AARGM) for the suppression of enemy air defense radar sites. Incorporating the tactics of when and how to use the HARM and AARGM missiles is a big part of the HAVOC training.

Supporting the air wing are the helicopter squadrons that come to NAWDC's rotary wing weapons school. The school provides shipborne tactics as well as high-altitude mountain flying training. The difference in air density between sea-level and mountainous terrain, as well as the winds aloft and unpredictability of weather at higher altitudes, requires aircrews to master flying helicopters in adverse conditions.

NAS Fallon and NAWDC's motto, "Train the way you fight, fight the way you train," will be engrained in the squadrons when they join their carrier on that next deployment. These are some of those squadrons and the colorful aircraft that have deployed to the high desert.

Opposite: The Knighthawks of VFA-136 were established on July 1, 1985, at their current home station of NAS Lemoore, California. Equipped first with the F/A-18A Hornet, in 1991 they would become the first fully operational night strike Hornet squadron when they received the Lot 13 F/A-18C. They completed their transition to the F/A-18E Super Hornet in June 2008, and have flown combat missions with it during Operation *Enduring Freedom* over Afghanistan and Operation New Dawn over Iraq. Making a return to Fallon on May 4, 2022, their CAG-bird, F/A-18E 166817/400, features a subdued outline of a hawk on its nose. The Knighthawks are currently assigned to Carrier Air Wing Seven (CVW-7) aboard the USS *George H. W. Bush* (CVN-77).

VFA-2 Bounty Hunters

With the callsign "Bullet," the VF-2 "Bounty Hunters" were established on October 14, 1972 at NAS Miramar, California, as the fourth fighter squadron to hold this designation. The Bounty Hunters would be equipped with 12 F-14A Tomcats for the next 20 years until 1993, when the squadron received the F-14D model. On its final carrier deployment with the Tomcat, flying from the USS *Constellation* (CV-64) in early 2003, VF-2 completed 483 combat sorties supporting Operation *Iraqi Freedom*. It would make the first use of the Joint Direct Attack Munition (JDAM) in combat, and ended with the deployment of 294 laser-guided munitions. On July 1, 2003, the squadron became VFA-2, receiving the F/A-18F Super Hornet, and relocating to its current home station of NAS Lemoore, California. It is currently assigned to Carrier Air Wing Two (CVW-2) aboard the USS *Carl Vinson* (CVN-70).

In the 20 years that the Bounty Hunters of VFA-2 have operated the F/A-18F Super Hornet, their carrier deployments have, for the most part, been outside of significant combat areas, as opposed to their F-14 Tomcat days when a number of deployments involved combat missions. The Bounty Hunters have changed their CAG-bird scheme very little over the years, and F/A-18F 166804/100 is currently serving in that role, wearing the squadron's traditional colors of red, white, blue, and yellow. (Jim Dunn)

It is rare to see two CAG-birds together, let alone when one is an F/A-18C Legacy Hornet, while the other is an F/A-18F Super Hornet. Less than four months after this September 11, 2017 mission, the "Blue Blasters" of VFA-34 would begin the final carrier deployment in the history of the Legacy Hornet. After returning from that deployment, F/A-18C 165403/400 would be assigned to the Marines in VMFA-232. (Jim Dunn)

VFA-14 Tophatters

The Navy recognizes VFA-14 as its oldest operating aviation squadron, with its lineage going back to September 1919. For the purposes of this brief history, we can begin with VA-14 being redesignated on December 15, 1949, as VF-14, equipped with F4U-4 Corsairs. After combat deployments off Vietnam with the F-4B Phantom II, and Operations *Desert Storm*, *Allied Force*, and *Enduring Freedom* with the F-14A Tomcat, VF-14 became VFA-14 on December 1, 2001, with the arrival of its F/A-18E Super Hornets. This would also see the "Tophatters" move to their current home of NAS Lemoore, California. Their first carrier deployment with the Super Hornet included combat missions in support of Operation *Iraqi Freedom*, and in 2004, they would be aboard the USS *Ronald Reagan* (CVN-76) for its maiden operational cruise. Currently, the Tophatters are assigned to Carrier Air Wing Nine (CVW-9) aboard the USS *Abraham Lincoln* (CVN-72).

Also known as "Fighting Fourteen," the current "Tophatters" CAG-bird F/A-18E 168927/200 is seen rolling out after landing at Fallon on September 27, 2021. Since going aboard the Navy's first aircraft carrier USS *Langley* (CV-1) in 1926, the squadron has flown nearly two dozen different types of aircraft on more than 20 Navy ships. No announcement has been made, but hopes are high that the F-35C will help the squadron remain the Navy's "Oldest & Boldest" long into the future. (Jim Dunn)

When the Navy announced a major reduction of F-14 squadrons in 1995, the Tophatters were not operating the version of the Tomcat that the Navy wanted to keep in service. Facing disestablishment, a campaign was launched to save the Navy's oldest squadron. In 1996, after having been transferred to another air wing, it has continued to serve even beyond its 90th anniversary, which was celebrated on their CAG-bird F/A-18E 166434/200 in 2009. (Jim Dunn)

VFA-27 Royal Maces

Known as the "Chargers," Attack Squadron Two Seven (VA-27) was established on September 1, 1967, and equipped with the A-7A Corsair II. Less than a year later, the unit would be on the first of its combat deployments off the coast of Vietnam with the A-7A. The Chargers would fly more than 2,500 combat sorties on their second cruise with this early model of the Corsair II. The squadron would make two more combat cruises with the A-7E, and continue to operate that aircraft until transitioning to the F/A-18A Hornet in January 1991.

VFA-27 continues to demonstrate skill in the attack role by delivering 18,000 lbs of ordinance on the night of January 13, 1993, over Iraq. The squadron would join CVW-5 in 1996, and relocate from NAS Lemoore, California to Naval Air Facility (NAF) Atsugi, Japan. In the process, the name was changed from the Chargers to the "Royal Maces." Now stationed at MCAS Iwakuni, Japan, VFA-27 is still assigned to Carrier Air Wing Five (CVW-5) aboard the USS *Ronald Reagan* (CVN-76).

Above: In October 2004, the "Royal Maces" transitioned to the Lot 23-24 F/A-18E Super Hornet, and then received the improved active electronically scanned array (AESA) radar-equipped Lot 34-35 F/A-18E, including their CAG-bird 168363/200, in February 2013. Though it has flown single-seat versions of both the Hornet and Super Hornet, VFA-27 has established a reputation as an air-to-ground attack specialist. In Operations *Enduring Freedom* and *Iraqi Freedom*, the squadron would fly hundreds of close air support missions, and make precision air strikes on a large variety of targets. (Jim Dunn)

Below: Returning to Fallon on a very hot August day in 2015, F/A-18E 168466/214 carries two air-to-air missiles, an AIM-9 Sidewinder and AIM-120 AMRAAM, along with an AGM-88 HARM for use against radar and surface-to-air (SAM) missile sites. Due to their being based in Japan, the "Royal Maces" and other squadrons assigned to CVW-5 do not get many opportunities to take advantage of the Fallon training experience, with visits only coming three to five years apart. (Jim Dunn)

VFA-31 Tomcatters

The "Tomcatters" of VFA-31 have the second longest official squadron lineage in the Navy. First established as VF-1B on July 1, 1935, and then combined with VF-8B on July 1, 1937 to form VF-6, the squadron would swap designations with VF-3 on July 15, 1943, this being the original "Felix the Cat" squadron. It would then become VF-3A on November 15, 1946, before being designated VF-31 on August 7, 1948. In 1972, the unit became the only Navy fighter squadron to achieve aerial victories in World War Two, Korea, and Vietnam. In 1980, the Tomcatters would conclude the longest association between a squadron and its assigned carrier after 24 years with the USS *Saratoga* (CV-60). The Tomcatters would fly the F-14 Tomcat from 1981 to its final official US Navy flight on October 4, 2006, then transition to the F/A-18E as VFA-31. Stationed at NAS Oceana, Virginia, VFA-31 is assigned to Carrier Air Wing Eight (CVW-8) aboard the USS *Gerald R. Ford* (CVN-78).

Felix the Cat has been the squadron mascot for 80 years, and VFA-31 CAG-bird F/A-18E 166766/100 has carried Felix on its tail for the last 17 years. During most of this period, the black tail with red trim has been the most favored, however, for a time in the mid-2010s, the color scheme was reversed with a red tail and black trim. (Jim Dunn)

Returning to Fallon from a sortie on December 4, 2017, F/A-18E 166786/112 displays an impressive scoreboard of combat missions from its most recent cruise. After being aboard the USS *George H. W. Bush* (CVN-77) for its maiden deployment in 2011, the Tomcatters are now preparing to be part of the maiden deployment of the USS *Gerald R. Ford* (CVN-78) in 2023. (Jim Dunn)

VFA-32 Swordsmen

First established on February 1, 1945, as Bombing Fighting Three (VBF-3) flying the F6F-5 Hellcat, the squadron was called the "Crazy Cats" as it was an offshoot of VF-3 "Felix the Cat." In 1946, the squadron would become VF-4A with F8F-1 Bearcats, and then VF-32 "White Lightning" with the F4U-4 Corsair in August 1948. Becoming the first fleet F8U-1 Crusader squadron in 1956, the squadron adopted the name "Fighting Swordsmen." With a combat record established in World War Two and Korea, the squadron would build one of the most extensive combat histories of any Navy organization. Using the callsign "Gypsy," it flew the F-4 Phantom II off Vietnam, the F-14A Tomcat in *Desert Storm* and subsequent operations that included the shooting down of two Libyan MiG-23s on January 4, 1989. Since November 2005, it has flown the F/A-18F Super Hornet as VFA-32. Currently based at NAS Oceana, Virginia, VFA-32 is assigned to Carrier Air Wing Three (CVW-3) aboard the USS *Dwight D. Eisenhower* (CVN-69).

The "Swordsmen" were part of the maiden cruise of the USS *Harry S. Truman* (CVN-75), beginning in November 2000, and during the next 14 years flew Tomcats and then Super Hornets on a number of combat operations from its deck. Their CAG-bird, F/A-18F 166661/100, is seen at Fallon on July 28, 2009, prior to their second carrier deployment with the Super Hornet. (Jim Dunn)

Nearly ten years to the day later, on July 29, 2019, F/A-18F 166661/100 was seen back at Fallon, working up for a cruise with CVW-3 aboard the USS *Dwight D. Eisenhower*. Since joining the "Ike" in 2015, VFA-32 has participated in more than 150 combat missions in the skies above Iraq and Syria, with 284,016lbs of precision-guided munitions placed on Islamic State (ISIS) targets. (Jim Dunn)

VFA-41 Black Aces

The fourth Navy squadron to be designated VF-41 was established at NAS Oceana, Virginia, on September 1, 1950, with the F2H-3 Banshee. In 1962, it would begin a 14-year period equipped with the F-4 Phantom II, conducting combat operations during the Vietnam War and peacekeeping missions in the Mediterranean. Converting to the F-14A Tomcat in 1976, the "Black Aces" would achieve several firsts, including the first air-to-air victories over two Libyan Su-22s in August 1981, plus, in 1995, the first use of laser-guided, air-to-ground weapons by the F-14, during Operation *Deliberate Force* over Bosnia. After giving up their Tomcats in 2002, the Black Aces would become the first operational F/A-18F Super Hornet squadron. Currently, VFA-41 is home stationed at NAS Lemoore, California, and assigned to Carrier Air Wing Nine (CVW-9) aboard the USS *Abraham Lincoln* (CVN-72).

Catching the last rays of sunlight as it takes to Runway 31L, F/A-18F 166842/100 proudly displays the squadron's motto "First to Fight, First to Strike" on its centerline tank. In May 2019, the Black Aces completed their final deployment aboard the USS *John C. Stennis* (CVN-74), a seven-month, around-the-world combat cruise that supported Operations *Enduring Freedom* and *Inherent Resolve*. Subsequently, this long-serving VFA-41 CAG-bird was reassigned to the "Flying Eagles" of VFA-122. (Jim Dunn)

Trying to determine how the lineage of Navy squadrons is recorded can be tricky. In 2015, VFA-41 gave its CAG-bird F/A-18F 166842/100 this 70th-anniversary scheme in recognition of the previous VF-41 that was commissioned on June 1, 1945. However, the Navy does not officially recognize this lineage, instead recording the squadron's date of establishment as September 1, 1950. (Jim Dunn)

VFA-83 Rampagers

The "Rampagers" trace their lineage back to the establishment of Naval Reserve Fighter Squadron VF-916 "Roaring Bulls" in April 1950, at NAS Squantum, Massachusetts. That squadron would be redesignated VF-83 on February 4, 1953, and then become VA-83 on July 1, 1955, with a change to the attack mission. Renamed the "Rampagers" in April 1957, the squadron has spent the vast majority of its carrier deployments in the Mediterranean Sea. A significant event during its service as an attack squadron came on April 15, 1986, when it employed the AGM-88 HARM in combat for the first time during Operation *El Dorado Canyon* in Libya. It would once again become a fighter squadron on March 1, 1988, as VFA-83 was equipped with the F/A-18C Hornet. Stationed at NAS Oceana, Virginia, since April 1998, the Rampagers are currently assigned to Carrier Air Wing Three (CVW-3) aboard the USS *Dwight D. Eisenhower* (CVN-69).

The "Rampagers" would be one of the last squadrons to transition from the Legacy Hornet to the Super Hornet. The squadron's first CAG-bird in the Super Hornet era, F/A-18E 166606/200, is seen in November 2019, taxiing out for a sortie with an AGM-154C-1 Joint Standoff Weapon (JSOW-C-1). This variant developed for the Navy is an unpowered guided bomb with a 500lb. warhead. It has a low-altitude launch range of 12 nautical miles (nm), extending up to 40nm when released at high altitude. (Jim Dunn)

During the Rampagers' first carrier deployment with F/A-18C Hornets, they flew 237 combat sorties in Operation *Desert Storm* from the deck of the USS *Saratoga* (CV-60). Wearing a liberal amount of the squadron's black and yellow colors, F/A-18C 165202/301 is seen on Fallon's MAT 1 ready for the CO of VFA-83. The Rampagers would conduct nearly 30 years of operations with the Legacy Hornet. (Jim Dunn)

VFA-86 Sidewinders

Tracing its lineage from Naval Reserve Fighter Squadron VF-921 that was called to active duty at NAS St. Louis, Missouri, on February 1, 1951, the squadron would become VF-84 on February 4, 1953, and then VA-86 with the F7U-3M Cutlass on July 1, 1955. Throughout the Vietnam War, it would conduct bombing missions from Yankee Station in the Tonkin Gulf with A-4E Skyhawks, and as the first Atlantic Fleet operational squadron with the A-7A Corsair II. The "Sidewinders" would once again become a fighter squadron as VFA-86 in June 1987, with its transition to the F/A-18C. The squadron would relocate to its current home of NAS Lemoore, California, and begin transitioning to the F/A-18E Super Hornet in July 2011. The Sidewinders are currently assigned to Carrier Air Wing Seven (CVW-7) aboard the USS *George H. W. Bush* (CVN-77).

The "Sidewinders" CAG-bird, F/A-18C 166060/200, is seen in February 2016 during its Fallon deployment ahead of a cruise as part of Carrier Air Wing Three (CVW) aboard the USS *Dwight D. Eisenhower* (CVN-69). This cruise would see the Sidewinders drop 330,000lbs of ordinance in support of Operation *Inherent Resolve*, which would bring VFA-86 another Battle "E," and the Wade McClusky Award for 2016. (Jim Dunn)

Even though VFA-86 calls California home, the "AG" on the tail denotes that for its most recent carrier deployments it has been assigned to an Atlantic Fleet air wing. Seen on April 25, 2022, during its most recent Air Wing Fallon deployment, the commanding officer's Super Hornet, F/A-18E 166951/301, has no color markings to distinguish this aircraft. In this case, the CO of VFA-86 is also the Deputy CAG for the air wing. (Jim Dunn)

VFA-87 Golden Warriors

Established on February 1, 1968, as VA-87 at NAS Cecil Field, Florida, the "Golden Warriors" would take their A-7B Corsair IIs into combat off of South Vietnam a little more than a year later. The squadron received its first F/A-18A Hornet on October 24, 1986, and simultaneously was redesignated VFA-87. The Golden Warriors flew 629 sorties during 43 days in Operation *Desert Storm*. Combat missions for the Golden Warriors were not confined to the Middle East as they employed their F/A-18Cs on August 30, 1995, for the first strikes of Operation *Deliberate Force* in Bosnia, and, in April 1999 in Kosovo, they flew 595 sorties in 68 days during Operation *Allied Force*. Due to heavy combat use, the squadron exchanged its F/A-18Cs for F/A-18A+ Hornets, and then later returned to the F/A-18C before getting the F/A-18E Super Hornet in 2015. Currently home-based at NAS Oceana, Virginia, VFA-87 is now with Carrier Air Wing Eight (CVW-8) aboard the USS *Gerald R. Ford* (CVN-78).

The training received with the Strike Fighter Advanced Readiness Program and the Air Wing Fallon deployments have paid major dividends for the "Golden Warriors" during the numerous carrier deployments that have involved combat during the last several years. This Fallon deployment in January 2019 shows a "War Party" of Golden Warriors being made ready for another mission, with its CAG-bird F/A-18E 168910/400 in the lead position. "War Party" is VFA-87's nickname and squadron call sign. (Jim Dunn)

On June 18, 2017, LCDR Michael Tremel, flying F/A-18E 168912/302, scored the first ever aerial victory for a Super Hornet by downing a Syrian Su-22 Fitter-K with an AIM-120 AMRAAM. When the Golden Warriors returned to Fallon in December 2017, F/A-18E 168912/302 sported an impressive tally from its recent carrier deployment that included an Iraqi flag with the silhouette of a Su-22 below it. (Jim Dunn)

VFA-94 Mighty Shrikes

Established at NAS Alameda, California, as VF-94 on March 26, 1952, the squadron was initially equipped with the F4U Corsair. It soon transitioned through a series of jet fighters before being assigned to the light attack mission equipped with the A-4 Skyhawk as VA-94 on August 1, 1958. It would fly combat missions throughout the Vietnam War with first the A-4 and then the A-7 Corsair II. During this period, the squadron officially became the "Mighty Shrikes." On March 8, 1962, it moved to its current home station of NAS Lemoore, California, and then returned to the fighter/attack role as VFA-94 in June 1990, flying the F/A-18C Hornet. Converting to the F/A-18F Super Hornet in 2015, VFA-94 is currently assigned to Carrier Air Wing Seventeen (CVW-17) aboard the USS *Nimitz* (CVN-68).

The orange and black colors of the "Mighty Shrikes" are now on striking display with the latest scheme on their CAG bird F/A-18F 168929/200, seen here during a three-week Strike Fighter Advanced Readiness Program deployment in February 2022 with an AGM-88 HARM under its left wing and an AIM-9 Sidewinder on the wingtip. The squadron would return to Fallon in the summer of 2022 to complete their five-week Air Wing Fallon deployment prior to their going aboard the USS *Nimitz* (CVN-68) for its next cruise. (Jim Dunn)

Illustrating how a CAG-bird scheme can change from one deployment to the next is this view from the tower at Fallon of the same VFA-94 Super Hornet, F/A-18F 168929/200, departing on a March 2020 sortie. The orange and black colors were represented in a much less bold fashion, with only the squadron symbol, the Shrike, standing out. With the Shrike being a predatory bird, it is only natural that this Super Hornet is outbound with both an AIM-9 Sidewinder on its left wingtip and an AIM-120 AMRAAM under its left wing. (Jim Dunn)

VFA-102 Diamondbacks

The "Diamondbacks" of VF-102 were established at NAS Cecil Field, Florida, on July 1, 1955, equipped with the F2H-4 Banshee. They would begin a 20-year association with the F-4 Phantom II in 1961 that would include flying combat missions over Vietnam from Yankee Station with the F-4J. The Diamondbacks would transition to the F-14 in 1981, and play a pivotal role in establishing the Tomcat as not only a great fighter but also a highly capable attack aircraft, while flying combat missions in Operations *Desert Storm* and *Enduring Freedom*. The squadron became VFA-102 with the transition to the F/A-18F Super Hornet in 2002 and, in November 2003, the squadron would be forward-deployed to NAF Atsugi, Japan. In 2018, VFA-102 relocated to MCAS Iwakuni, Japan, and in 2021, flew combat missions in support of the US withdrawal from Afghanistan. The Diamondbacks continue to be assigned to Carrier Air Wing Five (CVW-5) aboard the USS *Ronald Reagan* (CVN-76).

In 2010, VFA-102 received its second batch of Super Hornets equipped with the AN/APG-79 AESA radar, including its CAG-bird F/A-18F 166915/100, seen departing from Fallon's Runway 31R in August 2015. The Navy moved to end low-rate production of new Super Hornets in 2022, an effort coupled with the slow transition of the F-35C into the fleet that will force a number of front-line squadrons to maintain their currently assigned aircraft for a number of years. (Jim Dunn)

At the end of a very busy day, the Diamondbacks' 60th-anniversary Super Hornet rests on Fallon's MAT 2 ready for another morning sortie. For those few squadrons that have an aircraft with a modex number that corresponds to their squadron number, such as VFA-102's F/A-18F 166917/102, that aircraft will often be designated for unique markings to commemorate a person or special event in squadron history. (Jim Dunn)

VFA-103 Jolly Rogers

Established on May 1, 1952, as VF-103 "Sluggers" equipped with the FG-1D Corsair, the squadron would later be assigned the F-8 Crusader before beginning a nearly 20-year history with the F-4 Phantom II. During this time, it would score the first night-time victory over a North Vietnamese MiG-21, using an AIM-7 Sparrow missile. In 1995, when VF-84 "Jolly Rogers" was disestablished, the squadron adopted, though some insist it was forced to adopt, the "Jolly Rogers" name and traditions.

The squadron would fly the F-14 Tomcat from 1983 to 2005 in a number of combat operations from *El Dorado Canyon* to *Desert Storm* and *Enduring Freedom*. In February 2005, the "Jolly Rogers" became VFA-103 with the transition to the F/A-18F. They would continue to fly combat missions in support of Operation *Enduring Freedom*, *Iraqi Freedom* and *Inherent Resolve* with their Super Hornets. Currently home-based at NAS Oceana, Virginia, VFA-103 is assigned to Carrier Air Wing Seven (CVW-7) aboard the USS *George H.W. Bush* (CVN-77).

In 2018, the "Jolly Rogers" of VFA-103 celebrated the 75th anniversary of the establishment of the first Navy squadron to have that name by proudly flying the Jolly Roger flag on the tail of F/A-18F 168493/200. That first squadron was the famous World War Two VF-17, which would carry the name until their disestablishment in 1959, where upon VF-84 would take up the name until their own end in 1995. Note that inside the black band extending down from the cockpit are silhouettes of the aircraft flown by VFA-103 from the Corsair to the Tomcat. (Jim Dunn)

Returning to Fallon in April 2015, with a 2,000lb practice bomb under its left wing, the squadron commander's aircraft, F/A-18F 166621/201, carries the term "Mutha" on its tail to signify being named the fighter squadron with the highest "Fighter Spirit" for that year. This award began in the F-8 Crusader community in the 1950s, was then passed down through the Tomcat and now to the Super Hornet communities. (Jim Dunn)

VFA-113 Stingers

Established on July 15, 1948, at NAS San Diego, the "Stingers" of VF-113 were first equipped with the F8F Bearcat. Two years later, the squadron would receive the F4U Corsair and begin combat deployments during the Korean War. In March 1956, they would become Attack Squadron One One Three (VA-113) with the A4D Skyhawk, which they would take into combat in Vietnam before they transitioned to the A-7 Corsair II in December 1965. With the A-7, they continued their combat role in Vietnam including taking part in Linebacker II, the final major air campaign of the conflict, in late 1972. On March 25, 1983, the Stingers would become the first Navy fleet squadron to receive the F/A-18A Hornet, and was the first to become operational with it in December 1983. The Stingers would transition to the F/A-18E Super Hornet in 2016, at their current home of NAS Lemoore, California. They are currently assigned to Carrier Air Wing Two (CVW-2) aboard the USS *Carl Vinson* (CVN-70).

The Stingers would receive 12 new F/A-18E Super Hornets during 2016, including their CAG-bird 168877/200, seen returning to Fallon on April 26, 2021. During the first cruise after transitioning to the Super Hornet, VFA-113 carried out missions in support of both Operation *Inherent Resolve* and *Freedom's Sentinel*. (Jim Dunn)

Proudly displaying the squadron motto "First and Finest," F/A-18C 164257/300 is ready to take to Fallon's Runway 31L for a sortie in April 2014. The Stingers would set many safety records during their nearly 33 years of operating the F/A-18A/C Legacy Hornet, including being the first Navy squadron to achieve 100,000 mishap-free flight hours. After retirement from VFA-113, F/A-18C 164257 is now in the Marine Hornet training squadron VMFAT-101. (Jim Dunn)

VFA-115 Eagles

The lineage of the "Eagles" of VFA-115 is traced to the establishment of Torpedo Squadron VT-11 on October 10, 1942, flying Grumman TBF Avengers. After distinguished service in World War Two that saw its crews awarded seven Navy Crosses, the squadron was redesignated Attack Squadron VA-12A in November 1946. They would become VA-115 on July 15, 1948, and go on to another heavy period of combat with the AD Skyraider in Korea. The squadron called themselves the "Arabs," beginning in 1960, before entering another combat period in Vietnam, first with the A-1 Skyraider, then later with the A-6 Intruder. The unit became the "Eagles" in 1978, and then VFA-115 with the F/A-18C in 1996. The squadron would be the first fleet squadron to receive the F/A-18E Super Hornet in 2001. The Eagles are currently forward-deployed at MCAS Iwakuni, Japan, and are assigned to Carrier Air Wing Five (CVW-5) aboard the USS *Ronald Reagan* (CVN-76).

The current Super Hornet CAG-bird of VFA-115, F/A-18E 166859/300, is seen about to take off from Fallon with a 2,000lb Mk 84 general-purpose bomb carried on station three. The Eagles were the first to employ the Super Hornet in combat, flying 214 sorties on their first deployment in 2002. Now, all VFA-115 aircraft prominently display an eagle on their tail. (Jim Dunn)

The symbols featured on the tail of the Eagles' first Super Hornet CAG-bird F/A-18E 165781/200 are from the squadron's insignia that was adopted in 1956. Each of the five stars represent the major campaigns that the squadron has participated in, including World War Two, Korea, Vietnam, the First Gulf War and the Global War on Terror. The sundial is angled to show the time as 1:15. Today, F/A-18E 165781 is assigned to the "Fighting Omars" of VFC-12, the Navy's first Super Hornet adversary squadron. (Jim Dunn)

VFA-131 Wildcats

Though the "Wildcats" of VFA-131 trace their traditions back to World War Two, the squadron was officially established at NAS Lemoore, California, on October 2, 1983. In January 1985, they would move with their F/A-18A Hornets to NAS Cecil Field, Florida, to begin their long tour with the Atlantic Fleet. The Wildcats would fly the first ever combat missions for the F/A-18A Hornet in April 1986, against Libya during Operation *El Dorado Canyon*. In 1991, VFA-131 would complete the transition to the F/A-18C "Night Attack" Hornet. It would then make the maiden deployments of the USS *George Washington* (CVN-73) in 1994, and the USS *John C. Stennis* (CVN-74) in 1998, with Operation *Southern Watch* missions on both cruises. The squadron would transition to new F/A-18E Super Hornets in 2018, being one of the last fleet squadrons to retire its Legacy Hornets. Home based at NAS Oceana, Virginia, the Wildcats are currently assigned to Carrier Air Wing Three (CVW-3) aboard the USS *Dwight D. Eisenhower* (CVN-69).

Marking the "Wildcats'" initial visit to Fallon in July 2019, with their new Super Hornet CAG-bird, F/A-18E 168909/300, VFA-131 is preparing for a cruise with CVW-3 that will include missions over Afghanistan in support of Operation *Freedom's Sentinel*. This cruise would feature a new US Navy record of 206 consecutive days at sea without a port call. (Jim Dunn)

The VFA-131 CAG-bird, F/A-18C 165221/300, is seen at Fallon in February 2016, just prior to a six-month carrier deployment that would have the Wildcats flying 328 combat sorties over 2,200 hours, and expending 269 precision-guided munitions of 213,000lbs in support of Operation *Inherent Resolve*. This would be the squadron's final combat cruise in its more than 40 years of operating the F/A-18A/C Legacy Hornet. (Jim Dunn)

VFA-137 Kestrels

The "Kestrels" of VFA-137 were established on July 2, 1985, at NAS Cecil Field, Florida, to be equipped with the F/A-18A Hornet. In September 1992, VFA-137 would relocate to its current home of NAS Lemoore, California, and transition into the night attack-capable F/A-18C Hornet. In 2003, VFA-137 completed the final deployment of the USS *Constellation* (CV-64), participating in Operation *Southern Watch* and *Iraqi Freedom* with more than 500 combat sorties dropping more than 300,000lbs of ordnance. Upon return from this cruise, the squadron converted to the F/A-18E Super Hornet. The Kestrels are currently assigned to Carrier Air Wing Seventeen (CVW-17) aboard the USS *Nimitz* (CVN-68).

As the Navy's strike fighter squadrons slowly transition from the F/A-18E/Fs to the F-35C Lightning II, their Super Hornets are finding new homes in squadrons that were flying older models. After making its final flight as the CAG-bird with the Warhawks of VFA-97, F/A-18E 168867/300 is seen on February 7, 2022, returning to Fallon with a somewhat low-key scheme as the CAG-bird for the "Kestrels". In July 2022, the full complement of CVW-17 returned to complete its five-week Air Wing Fallon deployment prior to the next cruise aboard the USS *Nimitz* (CVN-68). (Jim Dunn)

After wearing a unique digital camouflage scheme for several years, F/A-18E 165897/00 is seen at Fallon in May 2014, proudly displaying a new CAG-bird scheme with the carrier's name, USS *Ronald Reagan*, in large letters across the spine. This glossy scheme would give way by April 2016 to the first version of a new look for the Kestrels. In an interesting turn, F/A-18E 165897/200 would be transferred to VFA-97 Warhawks to wear another aggressor digital scheme for a period prior to their transition to the F-35C. (Jim Dunn)

VFA-143 Pukin' Dogs

The official lineage for the "Pukin' Dogs" of VFA-143 begins on July 20, 1950, when the "Griffins" of VF-871, a Naval Reserve Fighter Squadron, were called to active duty at NAS Alameda, California. In February 1953, it became VF-123, and in April 1958, VF-53. On June 20, 1962, equipped with the F-4B Phantom II, the unit became VF-143 Pukin' Dogs. The squadron would soon take part in the first strike of the Vietnam War after the Tonkin Gulf Incident on August 5, 1964, in Operation *Pierce Arrow*. They would go on to make seven combat deployments during the conflict, achieving a MiG-21 kill on October 26, 1967.

In April 1975, VF-143 would complete the transition from the F-4J to the F-14A Tomcat, as well as moving to its current home of NAS Oceana, Virginia. On the Fallon ranges in May 1991, they would become the first Tomcat fleet squadron to drop live, air-to-ground ordnance. They became VFA-143 in 2005 with the conversion to the F/A-18E. The squadron is currently assigned to Carrier Air Wing Seven (CVW-7) aboard the USS *George H.W. Bush* (CVN-77).

In 2015, supporting Operation *Inherent Resolve*, VFA-143 conducted 390 combat missions totaling 5,673 hours, expending 422 precision-guided munitions with 369,616lbs of explosives. The success of a deployment such as this is due in large part to the training sorties flown over the three Fallon ranges, and here the squadron's current CAG-bird 168355/100 heads out on October 28, 2021, for yet another go. (Jim Dunn)

Squadron lore is that the "Pukin' Dogs" came by their unusual name when the squadron commander's wife stated that their Griffin looked more like a puking dog – something the crews readily accepted. For a time after the Tailhook scandal, the squadron was required to be known just as the "Dogs," but in time the unit was allowed to resume its full name. The Pukin' Dogs' previous CAG-bird, F/A-18E 166423/100, is seen ready to launch against a pair of VFC-13 aggressor F-5Ns in takeoff position on the parallel runway. (Jim Dunn)

VFA-146 Blue Diamonds

The squadron that is now VFA-146 "Blue Diamonds" was first established at NAS Miramar, California, as attack squadron VA-146 "Blacktails" on February 1, 1956. First equipped with the F9F-8 Cougar, the squadron would change its name to the Blue Diamonds in 1959, and then move to its current home at NAS Lemoore, California, on May 12, 1962. Conversion to the A-4C Skyhawk would see the Blue Diamonds conducting their next six deployments in combat operations off the coast of Vietnam. With another conversion, this time to the A-7E Corsair II, VA-146 would conduct the final Navy combat of the Vietnam War in early 1973. In 1989, the squadron would be designated VFA-146 and be equipped with the F/A-18C Hornet. This would be followed by the F/A-18E Super Hornet in 2015. The Blue Diamonds are currently assigned to Carrier Air Wing Eleven (CVW-11) aboard the USS *Theodore Roosevelt* (CVN-71).

The "Blue Diamonds'" first CAG-bird of the Super Hornet era, F/A-18E 165783/300, makes an early evening return to Fallon in February 2017. The squadron had just returned from a deployment that saw them fly 1,132 hours in support of Operation *Inherent Resolve* over Iraq and Syria, expending 92,000lbs of ordnance. They would also soon be trading their early Super Hornets for newer Lot 26 F/A-18E models. (Jim Dunn)

One of the most attractive CAG-bird schemes ever seen on a Hornet was displayed on F/A-18C 163740/300 of the Blue Diamonds. Being readied for another sortie in September 2010, VFA-146 would make its next deployment with CVW-14 aboard the USS *Ronald Reagan* (CVN-76), flying 212 combat hours in support of Operation *New Dawn* and *Enduring Freedom*. The Blue Diamonds had been flying combat missions in support of *Enduring Freedom* since December 2001. (Jim Dunn)

VFA-147 Argonauts

The "Argonauts" of VA-147 were established on February 1, 1967, at NAS Lemoore, California. The unit was the first operational A-7 Corsair II squadron, and the first to take that aircraft into combat. After ten years of operating the A-7E, VA-147 became the first squadron to receive the "Night Attack" model of the F/A-18C, becoming VFA-147 on July 20, 1989. In Operation *Desert Storm*, they would become the first to employ this version of the Hornet, along with being the first to use night-vision goggles. The Argonauts completed transition to the F/A-18E in February 2008, and were selected to become the first fleet squadron to receive the F-35C in January 2018. Currently assigned to Carrier Air Wing Two (CVW-2) aboard the USS *Carl Vinson* (CVN-70), VFA-147 completed the first operational carrier deployment of the F-35C in the first half of 2022.

Arriving at Fallon on May 4, 2022, for a consultation ahead of the Argonauts' next Strike Fighter Advanced Readiness Program deployment, F-35C 169636/402 clearly shows the effects from its just completed first ever operational carrier deployment. The salt air, combined with the heavy demands on an aircraft during a cruise, has taken a toll on the stealth coating that is critical to the mission of the Lightning II. What the Argonauts learned on this deployment will be of vital use to future squadrons that will be assigned the F-35C. (Jim Dunn)

The Argonauts' orange and black colors will likely never be seen on their F-35Cs. For the ten years that VFA-147 flew the Super Hornet, F/A-18E 166437/200 wore these colors as the squadron CAG-bird. This aircraft is now assigned to the Blue Diamonds of VFA-146. (Jim Dunn)

VFA-151 Vigilantes

The direct predecessor of VFA-151 is VF-23, established on August 6, 1948, at NAS Oceana, Virginia, with the F4U-5 Corsair. Named the "Flashers," the squadron would soon make three combat cruises in support of the Korean War, first with the Corsair, and another two with the F9F-2 Panther. In January 1959, they adopted the name "Vigilantes," and on 23 February 1959, at NAS Moffett Field, California, became VF-151. Seven combat cruises would be made with the F-4B and F-4N from NAS Miramar, California, during the Vietnam War. The unit transitioned to the F/A-18A Hornet, becoming VFA-151 on June 1, 1986, and delivered 817,000lbs of ordnance during Operation *Desert Storm*. At their current home of NAS Lemoore, California, they transitioned from the F/A-18C to the F/A-18E Super Hornet in February 2013. The Vigilantes are currently assigned to Carrier Air Wing Nine (CVW-9) aboard the USS *Abraham Lincoln* (CVN-72).

Previously assigned to the Knighthawks of VFA-136, the new CAG-bird of VFA-151 F/A-18E 166828/400 is now wearing the black and yellow colors of the Vigilantes. Returning to Fallon on March 24, 2021, the aircraft now features a large shark mouth to go along with its latest CAG-bird scheme. (Jim Dunn)

With a toned-down CAG-bird scheme, F/A-18E 168471/400 is seen returning to Fallon in June 2018. Training for combat also involves great risks, and on July 31, 2019, this aircraft would sadly be lost in a fatal crash that claimed the life of Lt. Charles Walker in the famous "Star Wars Canyon" in Death Valley National Park, California. (Jim Dunn)

VFA-154 Black Knights

While aboard the USS *Princeton* (CV-37) with their F9F-2 Panthers, the "Grand Slammers" of VF-837 were redesignated as VF-154 on February 4, 1953. When this squadron was assigned the F-8 Crusader in 1957, cartoonist Milton Caniff designed an insignia, leading them to become the "Black Knights". The squadron would have a significant 20-year history of operating the F-14A Tomcat from October 1983 to October 2003, when they transitioned to their current F/A-18F Super Hornets. During the Tomcat era, they would be the first forward based F-14 squadron when stationed at NAF Atsugi, Japan, and the first to deploy with an air-to-ground bombing capability that they would use supporting Operation *Iraqi Freedom*. Currently based at NAS Lemoore, California, VFA-154 is assigned to Carrier Air Wing Eleven (CVW-11) aboard the USS *Theodore Roosevelt* (CVN-71). Their next carrier deployment is scheduled for early 2024.

Lacking color and a weapons load, the latest CAG-bird for VFA-154, F/A-18F 169750/100, heads off from Fallon for a sortie on October 28, 2021. The aircraft does, however, carry markings denoting the Black Knights' 75th anniversary, as the squadron can date its official lineage back to Naval Reserve Squadron VFB-718, established on July 1, 1946, at NAS Floyd Bennett Field, New York. (Jim Dunn)

Equipped with the F/A-18F during the last 20 years, VFA-154 has continued to fly numerous combat missions in support of Operations *Iraqi Freedom* and *Enduring Freedom*. During this time, the Black Knights have also had at least three different F/A-18F Super Hornet CAG-birds, with the major difference in their schemes being whether or not they wore a black-painted fuselage spine. That striking scheme was last displayed here in February 2017, being worn on F/A-18F 166873/100. (Jim Dunn)

VFA-192 World Famous Golden Dragons

First established as VF-153 "Fightin' Kangaroos" at NAS Atlantic City, New Jersey, on March 26, 1945, the lineage would proceed to the VF-15A Black Knights on November 15, 1946, then to VF-151 on July 15, 1948, and finally becoming VF-192 at NAS Alameda, California, on February 15, 1950. Now known as the "Flying Dragons," the squadron saw extensive combat in the Korean War, flying F4U-4 Corsairs, before entering the jet age with the F9F-5 Panther. They then starred in two movies, *Men of the Fighting Lady* and *The Bridges at Toko-Ri*, with their Panthers receiving markings that resulted in their new name, "World Famous Golden Dragons." On March 15, 1956, the squadron became VA-192, and would fight the Vietnam War as an attack squadron, returning to a fighter mission as VFA-192 on January 10, 1986, with the F/A-18A. The Golden Dragons completed their transition to the F/A-18E Super Hornet in 2014, and are currently based at NAS Lemoore, California, with Carrier Air Wing Two (CVW-2) aboard the USS *Carl Vinson* (CVN-70).

The first Super Hornet CAG-bird for VFA-192, F/A-18E 165782/300, wears an attractive full-color scheme as seen in February 2016. The letters "SSHWFGD" on the centerline tank and top of the tail are the way the squadron wants everyone to know that they are the "Super Shit Hot World Famous Golden Dragons." This Super Hornet is also somewhat famous, as it is now assigned to the US Navy Blue Angels. (Jim Dunn)

The new CAG-bird for VFA-192, F/A-18E 169736/300, has taken on a much more modest look when seen here in March 2020. The Golden Dragons and the rest of CVW-2 have begun the cycle of deployments leading to their next cruise with a Strike Fighter Advanced Readiness Program at Fallon in September/October 2022, and an Air Wing at Fallon in the first half of 2023. (Jim Dunn)

VFA-195 Dambusters

The "Dambusters" trace their lineage to Torpedo Squadron VT-19 "Tigers," commissioned at NAAS Los Alamitos, California, on August 15, 1943. With its TBM Avengers, they took part in some of the largest battles in the Western Pacific. After World War Two, the squadron became VA-20A on November 15, 1946, and VA-195, flying the AD-2 Skyraider, on August 24, 1948. The squadron would become known as the Dambusters after its successful attack on the Hwachon Reservoir Dam in North Korea on May 1, 1951. The squadron flew A-4 Skyhawks and the A-7E Corsair II throughout the Vietnam War, becoming VFA-195 with the F/A-18A Hornet on April 1, 1985. The Dambusters were saved from being disestablished, and were instead transferred to CVW-5 with their first aircraft arriving at NAF Atsugi, Japan, in November 1986. Later with the F/A-18C in August 1991, and the F/A-18E Super Hornet from 2010, they would conduct combat missions in support of Operations *Desert Storm*, *Enduring Freedom* and *Iraqi Freedom*. The Dambusters remain with Carrier Air Wing Five (CVW-5), now at MCAS Iwakuni, Japan, and aboard the USS *Ronald Reagan* (CVN-76).

While being forward deployed with CVW-5 in Japan since 1986, VFA-195 has served aboard five different aircraft carriers, including making the final cruises for the USS *Midway* (CV-41) and the USS *Independence* (CV-62). On the last ever combat cruise for the *Midway*, the squadron would expend 356 tons of ordinance on 564 sorties during Operation *Desert Storm*, and record the first use of the Walleye II guided bomb delivered by a Hornet. (Jim Dunn)

Known as "Chippy Ho," F/A-18E 166901/400, the CAG-bird for the Dambusters has worn some of the most distinctive schemes in the Navy. The name comes from the squadron's call sign of "Chippy," hence when spotted the cry "Chippy Ho" sounds out. The squadrons of CVW-5 make only very rare visits to the United States, and their two deployments to Fallon for a Strike Fighter Advanced Readiness Program in February 2015 and the full air wing visit in August 2015 have not been repeated since then. (Jim Dunn)

VFA-213 Fighting Blacklions

Established on June 22, 1955 as VF-213 "Fighting Blacklions" at NAS Moffett Field, California, and equipped with the F2H-3 Banshee, the squadron would build a long combat record with three of the Navy's most recognized fighter jets. After a move to NAS Miramar, California, in 1961, they would transition to the F-4 Phantom in 1964, which would lead to flying 11,500 combat sorties and expending more than 6,000 tons of ordnance during the Vietnam War.

From 1976 to 2006, the Blacklions were assigned the F-14 Tomcat, taking part in Operation *Desert Storm*, *Desert Fox*, *Southern Watch*, and on October 7, 2001, leading the first strike on Afghanistan in Operation *Enduring Freedom*. After making the last operational flights of the F-14D, they transitioned into the F/A-18F and were redesignated VFA-213 on 2 April 2006. The squadron simultaneously moved to its current home of NAS Oceana, Virginia. Currently, VFA-213 is assigned to Carrier Air Wing Eight (CVW-8) where they will make the maiden deployment of the Navy's newest aircraft carrier, the USS *Gerald R Ford* (CVN-78).

The "Fighting Blacklions" continued to add to their combat history in the current Super Hornet era. In October 2008, they flew 680 combat sorties over 3,970 hours supporting Operation *Enduring Freedom*, and in 2014, on the maiden deployment of the USS *George H.W. Bush* (CVN-77), they conducted the first strikes of Operation *Inherent Resolve* against ISIS in Iraq and Syria. As seen on the tail of their CAG-bird, F/A-18F 166663/200, the name "McClusky" represents the Wade McClusky Award for the most outstanding Navy attack squadron in 2014. (Jim Dunn)

One deployment to Fallon that aircrew are excited about receiving is a selection to the famous TOP GUN course. The students will bring one of their squadron's aircraft, in this case F/A-18F 166678/213 from VFA-213, which has highlighted black markings that feature the names of the squadron's executive officer (pilot) and commanding officer (WSO) under the cockpit. It is seen on April 25, 2022, returning from a large class exercise that lasted just under one hour from takeoff to landing. (Jim Dunn)

VFC-204 River Rattlers

The "River Rattlers" of VFC-204 were established at NAS Memphis, Tennessee, on July 1, 1970, as VA-204, equipped with the A-4C Skyhawk. They would continue as an attack squadron after moving to NAS New Orleans, Louisiana, in 1978, with first the A-7B and then the A-7E Corsair II, until being redesignated as Strike Fighter Squadron (VFA) 204 on April 1, 1991. The squadron would convert to the F/A-18A/B Hornet in 1993, becoming the first Reserve Strike Fighter Squadron to serve in the adversary support mission for active-duty air wings. After nearly 30 years operating the Legacy Hornet, the River Rattlers began transitioning in 2022 to the F-5N, to continue its adversary mission. The squadron was redesignated VFC-204 at that time.

Though its long career ended with retirement to AMARG on June 29, 2022, F/A-18D 163457/414 from the "River Rattlers" of VFA-204, now VFC-204, wears one of the most recent adversary schemes now being applied to Navy and USAF aggressors. This pixelated aggressor or "Ghost" scheme is meant to mimic that on the latest Russian Sukhoi Su-57 stealth fighter. Seen here on Fallon's MAT 1 in May 2021, the "River Rattlers" were supporting the deployment of CVW-9 that included VMFA-314 flying the F-35C stealth fighter. (Jim Dunn)

Left: The former CAG-bird of the "Rampagers" of VFA-83, F/A-18C 164201/405 now wears a somewhat less colorful, though still unique scheme in its final service with VFA-204. Returning to Fallon on June 2, 2021, this Legacy Hornet is seen in another Su-57 scheme known as "Mako" for its shark-like appearance. It is likely that the schemes worn by these River Rattlers will soon be fading away as they begin their long stay at AMARG, which for 164201/405 began when it entered retirement there on April 11, 2022. (Jim Dunn)

Below: When F-5N 761578 became the first to receive the VFC-204 title and logo in early 2022, it was thought that the former Flagship of VFC-13 would quickly be headed to its new home in New Orleans. Mission requirements, however, have kept the F-5 at Fallon, as seen here as it returns from a flight on August 29, 2022. (Jim Dunn)

VAQ-130 Zappers

Originally established at NAS Agana, Guam, as VAW-130 on September 1, 1959, the "Zappers" are the oldest electronic warfare squadron in the Navy. First assigned the AD-5Q (EA-1F) Skyraider, the squadron would later gain the EKA-3B Skywarrior at its new home of NAS Alameda, California, being redesignated VAQ-130 on October 1, 1968. The squadron moved to its current home of NAS Whidbey Island, Washington, in 1974 while transitioning to the EA-6B Prowler. The Zappers completed their transition from the Prowler to the EA-18G Growler in February 2012, and are currently assigned to Carrier Air Wing Three (CVW-3) aboard the USS *Dwight D. Eisenhower* (CVN-69).

Touching down at Fallon after a sortie in July 2019 is *Robbie*, EA-18G 168268/500, the current CAG-bird for the "Zappers". During its first deployment with the Growler in July 2013, aboard the USS *Harry S. Truman* (CVN-75), VAQ-130 flew combat missions over Afghanistan, supporting Operation *Enduring Freedom*. More recently, they supported Operation *Inherent Resolve*, flying combat missions over Iraq and Syria. (Jim Dunn)

The Zappers' ground and maintenance personnel played a large role in helping the squadron to be recognized with the Navy Battle "E" award for superior performance and execution. Here, they prepare 168268/500 to receive its crew of pilot and electronic warfare officer (EWO) for a sortie on a cold February day at Fallon. (Jim Dunn)

Waiting on the Fallon ramp in July 2009, for its crew of pilot and three electronic countermeasures operators (ECMOs), EA-6B 163032/500 serves as the Zappers' final Prowler CAG-bird. During Operation *Desert Storm*, while flying from the USS *John F. Kennedy* (CV-67), VAQ-130 became the first Prowler unit to fire the AGM-88 HARM in combat. (Jim Dunn)

VAQ-137 Rooks

The first squadron to be designated VAQ-137, and to be known as the "Rooks," was established on December 14, 1973. Assigned the EA-6B Prowler, the Rooks would fly combat missions from the USS *America* (CV-66) during Operation *Desert Storm*. This first VAQ-137 would be disestablished on May 26, 1994, with the second VAQ-137 Rooks being re-established on October 3, 1996. The Navy, however, does not recognize a direct lineage between the two squadrons. Based at NAS Whidbey Island, Washington, the second VAQ-137 completed conversion to the EA-18G Growler in 2014, and is currently assigned to Carrier Air Wing One (CVW-1) aboard the USS *Harry S. Truman* (CVN-75).

It is unusual for a squadron to give their CAG-bird a different scheme to mark their participation in an exercise; however, that is what occurred when the "Rooks" gave their EA-18G 168266/500 CAG-bird this arctic scheme in 2018. Operation *Trident Juncture* saw the first carrier flight operations north of the Arctic Circle for the Navy in more than 30 years. Less than a month after returning home, the Rooks were at Fallon, taking part in a Strike Fighter Advanced Readiness Program deployment with CVW-1. (Jim Dunn)

The usual scheme worn on the Rooks' CAG-birds throughout the years feature a black-and-white checkerboard pattern, as seen on EA-6B Prowler 162934/500 and the current EA-18G Growler 168266/500. (Jim Dunn)

VAQ-141 Shadowhawks

The "Shadowhawks" were established in July 1987 at NAS Whidbey Island, Washington, and would soon make their maiden cruise aboard the USS *Theodore Roosevelt* (CVN-71) with CVW-8. From its second carrier deployment in 1991, with combat missions during Operation Desert Storm, the squadron would see combat on every carrier deployment they made for the next 21 years. In 2010, the Shadowhawks completed their transition from the EA-6B Prowler to the EA-18G Growler. Currently assigned to Carrier Air Wing Five (CVW-5) aboard the USS *Ronald Reagan* (CVN-76), the unit is the only permanently forward deployed VAQ squadron. VAQ-141 is based at MCAS Iwakuni, Japan.

In 2011, while assigned to CVW-2, VAQ-141 made the first Growler operational carrier deployment during the maiden cruise of the USS *George H.W. Bush* (CVN-77). This deployment would also see the first at-sea combat missions for the Growler, with a total of 237 sorties being flown in support of Operation *Enduring Freedom*. The Shadowhawks' CAG-bird, EA-18G 166928/500, carries an AGM-88 HARM as it departs on Runway 31R on a sortie in August 2015. (Jim Dunn)

Based in Japan since 2012 with CVW-5, VAQ-141 cross-decked from the USS *George Washington* (CVN-73) to the USS *Ronald Reagan* (CVN-76) in 2015, and changed home stations from Naval Air Facility Atsugi to MCAS Iwakuni in November 2017. (Jim Dunn)

The Prowlers of VAQ-141 were worked hard flying combat missions. In 2003, they conducted the first strikes of Operation *Iraqi Freedom*, flying more than 400 combat hours and launching 21 HARMs. This was followed in 2005 by more than 2,400 hours flown in direct support to ground forces from both the USS *Theodore Roosevelt* (CVN-71) and bases on shore. The squadron's Prowler CAG-bird 163529/500 is seen about to take Runway 31L for a Fallon sortie in June 2008. (Jim Dunn)

High Desert Deployment: Navy Colors on Display at NAS Fallon

VAQ-142 Gray Wolves

First established as the VAQ-142 "Grim Watchdogs" on June 1, 1988, the squadron made only one deployment before being disbanded in March 1991. They would return briefly from June 1991 to October 1993, as a detachment to VAQ-35, and then be re-established on April 3, 1997, as VAQ-142 "Gray Wolves." The unit was now a joint service expeditionary squadron that included United States Air Force (USAF) personnel who had served in the EF-111A. During the next 14 years, the squadron would forward deploy with its EA-6B Prowlers to fly combat missions from bases in Saudi Arabia, Turkey, Afghanistan and Iraq. In May 2011, the squadron would be selected to return to carrier aviation duties, and in July 2015, it would receive its first EA-18G Growlers. Currently home based at NAS Whidbey Island, Washington, VAQ-142 is assigned to Carrier Air Wing Eight (CVW-8) aboard the USS *Gerald R. Ford* (CVN-78).

The first Growler CAG-bird for the "Gray Wolves", EA-18G 168381/500 makes its return to Fallon in February 2017, with a scheme in the same style as worn by its Prowlers. The squadron made its first full carrier deployment with the Growler during the maiden cruise of the USS *Gerald R. Ford* (CVN-78) in late October 2022. (Jim Dunn)

Right: The final Prowler CAG-bird of VAQ-142 is seen in September 2012, returning to Fallon shortly after completing the squadron's first carrier duty in over 21 years. The Gray Wolves, as the next to last Navy Prowler squadron, would begin to retire their Prowlers in July 2014, with EA-6B 161245/500 going to AMARG on July 22, 2014. (Jim Dunn)

Below: When seen here in March 2019, about to sortie armed with an AGM-88 HARM, EA-18G 168381/500 is wearing a toned-down scheme in keeping with a policy of less color on VAQ CAG-birds. (Jim Dunn)

VAW-113 Black Eagles

The "Black Eagles" of VAW-113 were established on April 20, 1967, and immediately deployed to the Western Pacific with E-2A Hawkeyes in support of operations related to the Vietnam War. After providing support for Operation *Desert Shield* with its E-2C Hawkeyes, VAW-113 became the lead squadron for the introduction of the significantly improved E-2C Group II that included making its first deployment in 1994. The current home station for the Black Eagles is Naval Base Ventura County (NBVC) Point Mugu, California, with its current assignment being to Carrier Air Wing Two (CVW-2) aboard the USS *Carl Vinson* (CVN-70). In 2019, the unit transitioned from the E-2C HE2k Hawkeye 2000, becoming the first West Coast fleet squadron to operate the E-2D Advanced Hawkeye.

Seen here in April 2021 equipped with the E-2D Advanced Hawkeye, the squadron's new CAG-bird, E-2D 169070/600, features a red-eyed eagle and American flag in subdued outlines within the black nose markings. The Black Eagles have been playing a leading role in the introduction of the Advanced Hawkeye into the fleet, and with joint exercises involving the USAF and Marine Corps. (Jim Dunn)

The "Black Eagles" have displayed some of the most creative CAG-bird designs in the Navy. In April 2016, E-2C HE2K 165819/600 is seen featuring a silhouette of its carrier, the USS *Carl Vinson* (CVN-70), on its rear fuselage. Besides its many combat support missions, VAW-113 was awarded its tenth Navy Battle "E" for the role the squadron's Hawkeye 2000s played in providing airborne command and control for Operation *Tomodachi*, the relief efforts for the 2011 earthquake and tsunami in Japan. (Jim Dunn)

VAW-115 Liberty Bells

Established on the West Coast on April 20, 1967, the "Liberty Bells" quickly transitioned from the E-2A Hawkeye to the E-2B and began the first of its two combat deployments to the Tonkin Gulf during the Vietnam War. In September 1973, as part of Carrier Air Wing Five (CVW-5), they became the first forward-deployed Hawkeye squadron at NAF Atsugi, Japan. Flying from the USS *Midway* (CV-41), based in Yokosuka, Japan, the squadron would make 11 deployments throughout the Pacific and Indian Oceans before completing 179 combat sorties with its E-2Cs on *Midway's* final combat cruise, supporting Operation *Desert Storm*. In 2003, the squadron would fly combat sorties in support of Operations Southern Watch and Iraqi Freedom from the deck of the USS *Kitty Hawk* (CV-63), and in 2010 transitioned to the E-2C H2K Hawkeye 2000. The unit was reassigned to its current home of NBVC Point Mugu, California, in June 2017, and are currently assigned to Carrier Air Wing Eleven (CVW-11) aboard the USS *Theodore Roosevelt* (CVN-71).

Opposite: The Liberty Bells called Japan home for 44 years, from 1973 to 2017, and along with the other squadrons assigned to CVW-5 had some of the most memorable of all the Navy CAG-bird schemes. Displaying its green and yellow squadron colors, along with the flags of the United States and Japan, E-2C H2K 166505/600 is seen in its final CVW-5 CAG-bird glory, returning to Fallon in August 2015. (Jim Dunn)

Right and below: In 2019, the Liberty Bells returned to Fallon for their first full Fleet Readiness Training Program that included both an SFARP and Air Wing Fallon deployment. After completing a sortie on January 24, 2019, E-2C H2K 166508/602 folds its wings in preparation to enter the hot refueling pit, from which it will exit and return to its parking spot 26 minutes later, fueled for its next go. (Jim Dunn)

VAW-121 Bluetails

Established on April 1, 1967, at NAS Norfolk, Virginia, as VAW-121 "Griffins," the squadron was first assigned the Grumman E-1B Tracer, due to some carriers being unable to handle the larger E-2 Hawkeye. In July 1975, the unit would transition to the E-2C Hawkeye, and two years later deploy aboard the USS *Dwight D. Eisenhower* (CVN-69) for its maiden cruise. Changing the unit's name to the "Bluetails" in 1978, VAW-121 would be part of the then-record-setting 347-day cruise of the USS *Eisenhower* in 1980. In 2020, the Bluetails would be part of a nearly 10-month around-the-world deployment aboard the USS *Nimitz* (CVN-68). Currently VAW-121 is assigned to Carrier Air Wing Seven (CVW-7) aboard the USS *George H.W. Bush* (CVN-77).

Arriving back at Fallon on April 25, 2022, the "Bluetails'" CAG-bird, E-2D 169081/600, is one of the most recent Advanced Hawkeyes to enter service. The latest modification in the series is the addition of an aerial refueling capability, denoted by the probe above the cockpit. With this, the Navy can extend the current average four-hour flight to seven hours, going from two and a half hours on station to five hours. (Jim Dunn)

In 2014, VAW-121 became the second fleet squadron to be equipped with the E-2D, having previously operated the E-2C HE2K Hawkeye 2000. During Operation *Inherent Resolve* missions in 2017, they would be the first Hawkeye squadron since *Desert Storm* in 1991 to conduct defensive counter air (DCA) operations while carrying out missions over Iraq and Syria. (Jim Dunn)

High Desert Deployment: Navy Colors on Display at NAS Fallon

VAW-124 Bear Aces

Commissioned on September 1, 1967, at NAS Norfolk, Virginia, the squadron was first nicknamed "The Bullseye Squadron," with its first compliment of aircraft being four E-2A Hawkeyes. After several combat cruises in the Pacific for the Vietnam War, they returned to Atlantic Fleet operations that included being based out of Keflavik, Iceland, in December 1980. It was here, after directing a number of successful intercepts of Soviet Tu-95 Bear bombers, that the squadron was given the name "Bear Aces." The squadron added to its record of successful intercepts on August 19, 1981, when they directed two VFA-41 Tomcats in the downing of two Libyan Su-22s. With the E-2C, they would fly 331 combat sorties in support of Operation Desert Storm, direct combat strikes for Operation *Allied Force* over Kosovo, and direct the first strikes of Operations *Enduring Freedom* and *Iraqi Freedom*. The Bear Aces are home based at NAS Norfolk, Virginia, and currently assigned to Carrier Air Wing Eight (CVW-8) aboard the USS *Gerald R. Ford* (CVN-78).

The final E-2C H2K CAG-bird for the "Bear Aces", 166508/600, was one of the first aircraft to carry the USS *Gerald R. Ford* name when CVW-8 was assigned to the new carrier. Formerly with the Liberty Bells of VAW-115 as NH-602, it is seen returning to Fallon on March 24, 2021, just three months prior to the Bear Aces' conversion to the E-2D Advanced Hawkeye. (Jim Dunn)

In October 2013, the Bear Aces deployed to Fallon ahead of their 2014 cruise aboard the USS *George H.W. Bush* (CVN-77), which would see them flying 465 combat sorties in 2,120 hours, and being awarded the Battle "E" for their support of Operation *Inherent Resolve*. The squadron's CAG-bird at that time, E-2C Group 2 164353/600, would be retired to AMARG on August 26, 2015, receiving the honor of being parked on AMARG's "Display Row." (Jim Dunn)

HSC-8 Eightballers

The second Helicopter Anti-Submarine Squadron Eight (HS-8) was established on November 1, 1969, at NAS Imperial Beach, California. The "Eightballers" would make a number of deployments to support the Vietnam War with its SH-3D Sea King helicopters, before transitioning to the SH-3H to deploy for the Iranian hostage crisis and *Operations Desert Shield/Desert Storm*. On April 2, 1993, they completed transitioning to the new SH-60F Seahawk, and with it would support missions in Afghanistan for Operation Enduring Freedom. They would become the first in the Navy to be given the new HSC designation when they received the MH-60S on September 28, 2007, at its current home of NAS North Island, California. The Eightballers are currently assigned to Carrier Air Wing Eleven (CVW-11) aboard the USS *Theodore Roosevelt* (CVN-71).

Below and right: The primary mission for the Sikorsky MH-60S Knighthawk is search and rescue, vertical replenishment and anti-surface warfare. They are best recognized when serving as "plane guard" during aircraft operations aboard carriers. While serving with CVW-9, the "Eightballers" made several visits to Japan during their Western Pacific deployments, and its CAG-bird MH-60S 167869/0 is seen at Fallon in April 2011, with a scheme to mark its upcoming cruise. (Jim Dunn)

The first MH-60S CAG-bird for the Eightballers was 166307/0, with a scheme that left little doubt as to the name of the squadron. Movement of helicopters in helicopter sea combat (HSC) and HSM squadrons is common, with older airframes often going into training squadrons, as is the case with 166307 that is now serving with the Merlins of HSC-3, the MH-60S training squadron. (Jim Dunn)

HSM-73 BattleCats

The "BattleCats" were first established as Helicopter Anti-Submarine Squadron Light 43 (HSL-43) at NAS North Island, California, on October 5, 1984. Equipped with the SH-60B Seahawk, they were the first Navy squadron to become operational with the Light Airborne Multi-Purpose System (LAMPS) Mk. III, and the first to employ night vision goggles with LAMPS. The squadron would operate up to ten Seahawks in small detachments aboard frigates, destroyers, cruisers and aircraft carriers. With the transition to the MH-60R, the BattleCats became Helicopter Maritime Strike Squadron 73 (HSM-73) on February 1, 2012. In November 2016, HSM-73 would play a major role in providing support to relief efforts after the devastating earthquakes in New Zealand. The BattleCats are currently assigned to Carrier Air Wing Seventeen (CVW-17) aboard the USS *Nimitz* (CVN-68).

Opposite: For their primary mission of anti-submarine and anti-surface warfare, many consider the Sikorsky MH-60R "Romeo" to be the best helicopter in the world for these maritime missions. It is also very capable in its secondary duties of search and rescue and vertical replenishment, to name just two. The BattleCats' CAG-bird, MH-60R 167007/700, is seen getting attention from its crew on Fallon's MAT 7 during a deployment in April 2014. (Jim Dunn)

Below and right: During the 2010s, Navy HSC and HSM squadrons had some of the most colorful and distinctive CAG-bird schemes in the fleet. At the huge Centennial of Naval Aviation event in 2011 at NAS North Island, several of the squadrons proudly displayed their CAG-birds for the public. Today, many of these schemes have been toned down or eliminated when the aircraft went through depot-level maintenance. Today, MH-60R 167007 is with HSM-71, showing no color at all. (Jim Dunn)

CHAPTER FOUR
SAINTS AND OTHER SINNERS

NAWDC has been home to VFC-13, the Fighting Saints, since the move was made from Miramar to NAS Fallon in 1996. During the air station move, VFC-13 took over the adversary mission from VFA-45 and VFA-127. Simultaneous to the move, the Fighting Saints transitioned to the Northrop F-5E Tiger II, and from December 2022, the squadron is now flying F-16C Block 32 Fighting Falcons. The F-16s received by VFC-13 are all ex-Arizona Air National Guard aircraft.

The F-5Es are today flying with VFC-204 "River Rattlers" based at Naval Air Station/Joint Reserve Base New Orleans, Louisiana.

Better adversaries require increased training and combat readiness of US forces. Moving to the F-16C Block 32 enables the Fighting Saints to provide an increasingly realistic threat to Navy and Marine Corps air crews. The F-16s supply a threat capable of engaging or entering the battlespace at altitudes above 50,000ft, can fly at more than 800 knots (920.6mph), and maneuver at more than 9 Gs.

Opposite, below and overleaf page: For more than 25 years, the Fighting Saints of VFC-13 have provided adversary support at NAS Fallon with their colorful F-5E/F, and now F-5N Tiger II aggressors. With former USAF F-16Cs now arriving at Fallon, and VFC-13 making the transition from Tiger IIs to Vipers, it remains to be seen which of the many aggressor paint schemes used by the "Saints" are going to be applied on their "new" jets. While the "Banana" or "Rotten Banana" F-5N 761536/02 had already given up this scheme when it moved on to the Marines of VMFAT-401, the other Tiger IIs such as F-5N 761535/14 will also be leaving Fallon soon, with boring grey jets likely replacing them. (Jim Dunn)

High Desert Deployment: Navy Colors on Display at NAS Fallon

The ex-Air National Guard F-16s have been upgraded during their service in Arizona with the Center Display Unit, the Scorpion Helmet Mounted Display, Northrop Grumman's Litening advanced targeting pod and the AN/APG-83 Scalable Agile Beam Radar–Active Electronically Scanned Array radar. In the cockpit, the center display unit, with its six-by-eight-inch display, displays greater detail and information from both the Litening pod and the radar.

In addition to the aircraft of the Fighting Saints, the US Navy contracts with outside vendors who provide dissimilar adversary threat aircraft. Three companies are active in this space including Tactical Air Support, more commonly known as "TacAir" that today provides services at NAS Fallon. In addition, Airborne Tactical Advantage Co., which is known in industry by the acronym ATAC, has served the Department of Defense for nearly 30 years, as well as Draken International, a company that flies L-159E Honey Badgers to train crews, in particular back-seaters, in air-to-ground munitions deployment. The civilian service providers fly a mix of adversary aircraft from the F-16, Mk-58 Hawker Hunter and Mirage F1 to the F-21 Kfir, F-5 Advanced Tiger, A-4 Skyhawks, L-39 Albatros and L-159Es.

Each of the civilian contractors provides aggressor aircraft for air-to-air training, including air-to-air gunnery and fighter intercepts as part of an airborne engagement. ATAC and TacAir also engage E-2 Hawkeye controllers and EA-18G Growler weapon systems operators and aircrew on how to counter enemy electronic warfare operations flying in the airborne battlespace.

This deadly combination of military and civilian aggressor aircraft can offer unique challenges to the air wing squadrons deploying to Fallon. Here, VFC-13 F-5N 761564/01 leads Israeli-built Kfir-C2 N402AX, from Airborne Tactical Advantage (ATAC), out for another sortie against a group of Super Hornets. Besides the Kfir, Fallon has seen a wide variety of civilian-operated aggressor aircraft over the years including, the A-4 Skyhawk, Hawker Hunter, L-29, L-39, T-33, and most recently, the F-5AT Advanced Tiger. While the Kfir is no longer a regular adversary at Fallon, it will be remembered not only for its great appearance but, more importantly, for leading the way for civilian aggressor aircraft operating from Fallon. (Jim Dunn)

One of the first civilian companies to provide tactical fighter aircraft to support military adversary training requirements is Draken International, based in Lakeland, Florida. This company operates a number of fighter types in both the US and Europe, including the Mirage F-1 and the soon to enter service F-16 Fighting Falcon, and one of its longest-serving aircraft is the A-4 Skyhawk. Built as A-4F 155052, this Skyhawk also served in the Royal Australian Navy as A-4G 871, and as upgraded A-4K NZ6215 for the Royal New Zealand Air Force. Recently, N145EM has received a new 'Ghost' scheme, enabling it to evolve in the ever-changing world of adversary tactics. (Jim Dunn)

Based at nearby Stead Field outside of Reno, Nevada, Tactical Air Support (TacAir) has the current contract to supply adversary support to the Navy at Fallon. To meet this contract, TacAir is using upgraded F-5E/Fs obtained from the Royal Jordanian Air Force and now designated F-5AT Advanced Tigers. Flying with the call sign "Villain," former F-5E serial number 77-1777, now F-5AT N647TA, TacAir 06, returns from another engagement over the Fallon ranges. (Jim Dunn)

The two-seat Northrop F-5F Tiger II is a valuable asset to both the Navy and civilian contractors such as TacAir. Many of the pilots flying adversary aircraft for TacAir are former graduates of TOP GUN or the Fighter Weapons School, and the F-5F provides the training aircraft needed to not only familiarize crews with the F-5, but also to introduce them to the technical advances in these aircraft. Wearing a sleek two-tone scheme, F-5F s/n 79-1918, N699TA, TacAir 21, is seen about to depart Fallon for the short flight back to Stead Field. (Jim Dunn)

Right and below: Civilian contractors are also deploying aircraft to Fallon for roles other than adversary support for fighter squadrons. The three ranges at Fallon support other types of essential training. To train controllers in the close air support mission, Draken International dispatched a pair of L-159E "Honey Badgers" capable of dispensing ordnance, along with a pair of camera-equipped L-39s to provide some of the aerial assets needed for this training. Seen returning after a June 1, 2022 sortie are Draken International L-159E N270EM and Coastal Defense Inc. L-39 N139JK. (Jim Dunn)

Opposite and above: Difficulties in obtaining suitable low-time F-5Fs led the Navy to commission the creation of three "Franken Tigers," an aircraft that mates the two-seat forward fuselage of an F-5F to a low-time F-5E from the Swiss Air Force. Seen in these images from February 2022, the Fighting Saints F-5F Franken Tiger 761580/20 is being given a workout that includes the rare use of the drag chute on Fallon's very long, 14,000ft Runway 31L. The next time this Franken Tiger is seen at Fallon, it will likely be in VFC-204 markings. (Jim Dunn)

Above and opposite: Ever since portraying the villainous black "MiG-28" in the original 1986 *Top Gun* movie, a black-painted F-5 aggressor has been a fixture in the Navy adversary program. Today, that role at Fallon is played by F-5N Tiger II 761578/13 from the "Saints" of VFC-13. The question is, will another example of the black jet emerge when the Saints transition from their long-serving F-5s to the F-16 Fighting Falcon? This transition is under way, with F-5N 761578/13 having transferred to New Orleans with the River Rattlers of VFC-204. (Jim Dunn)

Opposite and above: NAWDC and its predecessors have been the only Navy organizations to be equipped with the F-16 since 2002. At that time, 14 F-16A/B Block 15 models, 12 of which were embargoed Pakistani Air Force aircraft stored at AMARG, became aggressors to augment the F/A-18A/B Hornets operating at Fallon. Here, a crew is about to board one of the four ex-Pakistani B models, 920460/06, while another B model, 902458/04, is viewed from the Fallon tower returning from an afternoon sortie. (Jim Dunn)

Above and opposite: While the current "Viper" F-16A/Bs don't match the performance characteristics of the former short-lived "hot rod" F-16N model that the Navy had specifically built for them in the late 1980s, they more than make up for it in the capabilities of their radar and other systems (F-16A 920408 is seen departing). The Navy began receiving its third group of F-16s starting in 2022, this time 26 C/D models from the USAF and the Air National Guard, of which 12 F-16C Block 32s are slated to replace the F-5s in VFC-13, and eight F-16Cs and six F-16D Block 25s going to NAWDC to join the F-16s currently assigned. The first of the VFC-13 "Vipers" is 860239/301, seen departing for a mission at Fallon on October 26, 2022. (Jim Dunn)

Above and opposite: The last stand of the Legacy Hornet in the US Navy is in its final stages with NAWDC at NAS Fallon. Aircraft such as F/A-18C 164646/37, known as the "Gazelle," and F/A-18C 164630/47 with this Arctic Splinter scheme, are in the last cadre of Navy Hornets. With decades of service supporting the missions at Fallon, these Hornets will be replaced in their roles by the incoming F-16C/Ds, as well as additional Super Hornets and F-35s when they become available. (Jim Dunn)

Left and below: Even though full-rate production of the Super Hornet began more than 25 years ago, you won't find any examples currently in storage at AMARG. In a perfect world, organizations like NAWDC would be able to replace their Legacy Hornets with older model Super Hornets at the appropriate time; however, there are just not enough Super Hornets to fulfill the need. This also means that those older model Super Hornets such as F/A-18F 166805/104, formerly of VFA-211, will need to be kept in service for many years to come in order to meet the demand. A rare exception to this came in 2022, when NAWDC received F/A-18F 169974/130, a brand new Block III Super Hornet that is seen here departing for a mission on October 3, 2022. (Jim Dunn)

CHAPTER FIVE
SENTINELS OF THE PAST

Greeting visitors as they enter Fallon on the Reno Highway is A-7E Corsair II 159647/01, which saw service with the "Hellrazors" of VA-174, the "Valions" of VA-15 and the Golden Dragons of VA-192 before its last assignment with the Naval Strike Warfare Center at NAS Fallon. (Jim Dunn)

High Desert Deployment: Navy Colors on Display at NAS Fallon

NAS Fallon's gate guards and heritage air park represent US Navy and Marine Corps aviation from the late 1940s through the new millennium, with examples of many frontline combat aircraft. Aircraft introduced in the 1940s and '50s are covered by the F-86 Sabre and AD-4B Skyraider, while the 1960s-era aircraft that fought through the Vietnam War and served to project America's might during the Cold War are seen in the A-4 Skyhawk, A-5 Vigilante, A-7 Corsair II and the supersonic-capable F-4 Phantom II and F-8 Crusader (technically introduced in 1957). The Navy's first supersonic multi-role fighter, the F-14 Tomcat, is on display as well.

The air park also includes examples of jet fighters flown by America's Cold War adversaries. The F-86 Sabre's nemesis, the Mikoyan-Gurevich MiG-15, is represented by a Polish-built version known as the Lim-2. The MiG-21 was a fierce combatant during the Vietnam War and was a mainstay of most Soviet-bloc nations through the 1960s to the 1990s. The example on show last served with the Hungarian Air Force.

Displayed alongside the MiG-21 is an ex-East German Air Force MiG-23ML, NATO code name Flogger. Like the F-14, the MiG-23 has variable-geometry, or swing wings, that enable better low-speed handling at slow speeds, and improved aerodynamics at supersonic speeds. The MiG-23ML is a second generation, lightweight version of the Flogger and was capable of accelerating to Mach 2.1 in full afterburner.

Contemporary to the F-14 Tomcat is the Soviet MiG-29 Fulcrum, which still serves as a frontline fighter for many nations. MiG-29s are today flown by numerous Soviet successor states, Ukraine, India, Peru, and Serbia among other nations. The United States obtained a number of MiG-29s and, along with previous generations of Soviet fighters, evaluated the combat capabilities of these fighters. Tactics were developed and disseminated throughout the USAF, Navy and Marines.

Displaying both the American and Soviet aircraft in the heritage air park enables design and size comparison of each nation's aerial adversaries while showing the evolution of Navy and Marine Corps fighters.

Hidden away from the air park is the NAWDC boneyard, where half a dozen legacy F/A-18 Hornets reside. These jets had served as a parts source and long ago donated their General Electric F404 engines to keep other Hornets in the air. At some point in the near future, one of the residents of the base boneyard will most likely end its days in the heritage air park.

The storied history of NAS Fallon would not be complete without a mention of its search and rescue squadron. When the call went out for the "Longhorns," the unit would respond within half an hour if the field was open, and an hour if it was closed. This applied to both military and civilian calls for assistance. Having an MH-60S Knighthawk, such as "Longhorn 04" 166296/04, ready on short notice was an important mission that NAWDC faces a big challenge replacing as the "Longhorns" were disestablished in April 2022. Now, MH-60S 166296/04 has become 166296/70 with NAWDC. (Jim Dunn)

Mounted on poles just to the left of the main entry gate at Fallon are two former attack jets wearing markings of Fallon-based aircraft. Last serving with the River Rattlers of VA-204 at NAS New Orleans, Vought A-7B Corsair II 154420 was struck off charge on October 12, 1983. For Douglas A-4B Skyhawk 142100, its career ended after serving in two unique, short-lived Anti-Submarine Warfare Fighter Squadrons, VSF-1 and VSF-3, both based at NAS Alameda, California. It was stricken from the inventory on Oct. 21, 1969. (Jim Dunn)

One of the gate guards at NAS Fallon is the oldest, and the only piston-engine aircraft on display. There were 165 examples of the Douglas AD-4B Skyraider built with the capability to deliver a nuclear weapon, and one AD-4B set a world record for the heaviest payload carried by a single-engine, piston-powered aircraft. The Skyraider was a workhorse of the Korean and Vietnam Wars, and after its Navy service, AD-4B 132261/500 finished its career with the Marines of VMA-121. It is displayed in the markings of VA-152 aboard the USS *Oriskany* (CV-34). (Jim Dunn)

Another of Fallon's gate guards is North American RA-5C Vigilante 156638/207. One of 69 built specifically to be a high-speed reconnaissance platform, this Vigilante was delivered in August 1970, to Reconnaissance Attack Squadron Five (RVAH-5) aboard the USS *Enterprise* (CVN-65). By August 1979, its career was over, and it was first retired to Naval Air Weapons Station (NAWS) China Lake. Later, it was transferred to Fallon for display, where it is now painted in a Vietnam-era camouflage scheme from RVAH-6 aboard the USS *Constellation* (CV-64) to represent its service during that conflict. (Jim Dunn)

The Chance Vought F8U Crusader looks like it was designed specifically to be adorned with a shark mouth. Built as F8U-1E 145449, this Crusader was redesignated in 1962 as an F-8B, and later, after new radar and the addition of underwing hardpoints, became an F-8L. It ended its career as a DF-8L drone controller at NAWS China Lake, from where it would be saved. This Crusader is displayed in the colors of the "Sundowners" of VF-111. (Jim Dunn)

Like many of the aircraft on display in Fallon's Air Power Park, F-14A Tomcat 159626 is on loan from the National Museum of Naval Aviation at NAS Pensacola, Florida. Retired after a relatively short career in 1987, having last served with the "Checkmates" of VF-211, this Tomcat is now painted in the colors of the Bounty Hunters of VF-2 during its long association with the USS *Ranger* (CV-61). Aircraft from *Ranger* flew more than 500 combat missions in support of Operation *Desert Storm*. (Jim Dunn)

Built by McDonnell as F4H-1 151510, and redesignated as F-4B-20-MC in 1962, this Phantom II has the distinction of having been displayed on both a U.S. Air Force and a U.S. Navy installation. After being retired on September 29, 1977, 151510 became F-4C 63-7411 for display at Luke AFB, Arizona, before the National Museum of Naval Aviation moved it to Fallon, where it was then displayed as F-4S 151510/100 from the Chargers of VF-161 aboard the USS *Midway* (CV-41). (Jim Dunn)

Perhaps the best way that a former USAF fighter jet can find its way to display status at a Navy installation is for it to have been flown by a naval aviator, or, in the case of this F-86F Sabre, by a famous Marine aviator. In July 1953, Marine Corps Maj. John Glenn, known as the "MiG Mad Marine," scored three MiG kills while on temporary duty with the 25th Fighter Interceptor Squadron in F-86F 52-4584. Although painted as 52-4584, the serial number for this F-86F is unknown. It is most likely a former Navy QF-86F drone. (Jim Dunn)

In the mid-1950s, **PZL Mielec** in Poland built approximately 500 examples of the Russian MiG-15bis, which was an improved version of the original MiG-15 made famous during the Korean War. Designated Lim-2, this version saw service in Poland and numerous air forces in the Soviet sphere. Former Polish Air Force Lim-2 #1614 is the oldest of the Soviet-era jets on display at Fallon, and is now wearing this Korean People's Army Air Force (North Korea) camouflage scheme as MiG-15bis #546. (Jim Dunn)

When Moldova was freed from the Soviet Union in 1992, it inherited the 86th Guards Maritime Fighter Aviation Regiment. This unit had been the first in the Soviet Naval Air Forces to operate the MiG-29 Fulcrum. Due to the total inability to either fly or maintain these fighters, the decision was made to dispose of them as soon as possible. In 1997, a number were purchased by the United States government, and it is believed that this MiG-29 is one of those aircraft. (Jim Dunn)

After German reunification, the Luftwaffe gained a variety of Soviet aircraft from the former East Germany. Based at Peenemünde with JG-9, MiG-23ML Flogger #353 was taken on as 20+23 by the Luftwaffe. Its service was brief, and eventually it found its way to the NAS Fallon Airpark. (Jim Dunn)

Produced in greater numbers than any other supersonic fighter – nearly 12,000 – and serving in more than 50 air forces since its introduction in 1960, the Mikoyan-Gurevich MiG-21 Fishbed is the most recognizable of all the Soviet-era jet fighters. Assigned to the "Kapos" Tactical Fighter Wing at Taszar, Hungary, from 1975 to 1997, MiG-21bis Fishbed L #3964 now represents one of the best adversary aircraft that Navy pilots have ever engaged. (Jim Dunn)

The end of the line. On a corner of the NAWDC ramp, these seven F/A-18C Hornets are awaiting their fate in what passes as the Fallon boneyard. All of these Legacy Hornets have already given up their engines and many other parts to help keep the few remaining Hornets assigned to NAWDC flying. Eventually, they are going to be scrapped on base, or trucked out for final disposal. Each has served a long career through both times of peace and periods of conflict. (Jim Dunn)